T0149383

OTHER PUBLICATIONS BY ALLEN R. REMALEY

Ya Should'a Been There!

Allen R. Remaley

authorHOUSE®

AuthorHouse™
1663 Liberty Drive
Bloomington, IN 47403
www.authorhouse.com
Phone: 1 (800) 839-8640

© 2018 Allen R. Remaley. All rights reserved.

No part of this book may be reproduced, stored in a retrieval system, or transmitted by any means without the written permission of the author.

Published by AuthorHouse 11/14/2018

ISBN: 978-1-5462-6817-8 (sc)
ISBN: 978-1-5462-6816-1 (e)

Library of Congress Control Number: 2018913540

Print information available on the last page.

Any people depicted in stock imagery provided by Getty Images are models, and such images are being used for illustrative purposes only. Certain stock imagery © Getty Images.

This book is printed on acid-free paper.

Because of the dynamic nature of the Internet, any web addresses or links contained in this book may have changed since publication and may no longer be valid. The views expressed in this work are solely those of the author and do not necessarily reflect the views of the publisher, and the publisher hereby disclaims any responsibility for them.

DEDICATION

To all those who might have thought
that paying attention and completing
assignments was worth it. And, of
course, to my wife and children, all of
whom make my life worth living.

AUTHOR'S PREFACE

Before any writing takes place, whether it be a novel, short story or any other piece of recorded history, the writer should ask some questions. "Will the story portray some aspect of the past, present or future?" "Will the work reflect realism as observed by others?" "Is the document worthy of reading, i.e., will the reader find it interesting?" And, most importantly, "Will the author enjoy putting the piece together in a presentable format; will it please the writer?" If at least half of the answers to those questions are positive, the writer should make the effort to record, if not for personal reasons, then for the simple fact that someone might react to the work and opine silently or more openly to others about what has been read. In my estimation, in this story, all the answers to the above questions are, "Yes". That being said, let's look at the topic of interest.

In one's lifetime, if a drive to achieve above the norm exists within the soul, mind and body of an individual, things happen which should be documented. The missteps, the hurdles overcome, the happenstances of one's actions and the more-interesting events of one's life might be set to type and be worth an afternoon or evening's read. This story is about a teacher's desire to make his subject come alive for his students. But, perhaps the real reason for the teacher's motivation had to do with his fear, his fear of failure in the eyes of others. The protagonist in this tale is a person who grew up without the privilege of wealth, position and social standing. Surrounded by others more blessed with the right stuff, and a clear pathway to a better future, this individual had to find the ways to overcome what he thought to be the yoke of inopportunity. This is an account of a boy's wanting to succeed in life, and he wanted to share what he had learned along the way with those in his classroom. And, in the end, it, this testament, is a portrayal of those students and their experiences which cement the idea that the teacher might have achieved his goal. "Ya Should'a Been There."

CHAPTER 1

Hand-Me-Down-Shoes

For Floyd Sarvey, it would be hard to pinpoint just what made him feel inferior to those around him. It didn't seem to be the little shack he and his mother shared---a two-room shed used by his grandmother to store her gardening tools---lawnmower and odds and ends collected over decades. Once his grandmother, the woman who loved him unconditionally, realized that Floyd's mother, her daughter, needed help because of a husband who had jumped on a boxcar and rode the rails all the way to Texas to pursue better fields of opportunity, the little two-room collect-all was offered as a place of refuge.

No indoor plumbing. A two-seater outhouse stood close by for grandmother, her two boarders and now, her daughter and grandson. Other than a coal-fired cook stove, no heating would warm mother and son during the cold Western Pennsylvania winters. A single electric line was strung from the grandmother's home to the little house, and this third-world country-hookup allowed for a lamp in each of the two rooms to light the interior. Never once did Floyd complain about his living conditions. A WWII army cot served as his bed, and grandmother's handmade quilts provided a cocoon-like warmth for the little boy who thought he was so fortunate to live in such a place.

Floyd's feelings of inadequacy came from other things. Floyd's mother had an older sister who had escaped the poverty of a town fueled by coal mines and weighted down by beer-selling taverns which catered to men suffering from black-lung disease and women who had little opportunity to supplement the wages of their husbands. Floyd's aunt had moved to a larger town down river along the Susquehanna. There, she married a man who respected her, treated her kindly and gave her two children. The husband and wife then started a beauty salon, and in a short time, the two became the town's leading hairdressers. The income that business provided set them apart from a dismal past, and, to some degree, Floyd was to benefit.

Floyd soon became aware that he had two older cousins. On irregular visits to her mother up river, Floyd's aunt and her husband would arrive driving a big, new car and unload boxes of used boys' clothing and shoes. Those shoes, always run over at the heels, and not always the appropriate size, served Floyd through high school. He never once complained about blisters or scuff marks left on heavily-used leather. In school, Floyd kept his feet crossed under his desk so as to hide the run-over heels. Other than a pair of P.F. Flyers, his required footwear for gym class, Floyd never had a pair of his own shoes until Marine Corps boot camp. But, it was the sneakers which helped Floyd climb the first rung of the ladder leading upward in respectability. Floyd was an athlete.

In gym classes in high school, Floyd's ability on the hardwoods came to the attention of the football coach. By the end of his senior year in high school, he had earned All County and All-District first-team recognition. At the time, smash-mouth football in Western Pennsylvania was popular, and Floyd was not one to back down from any challenge on the field or off. But, size was still important. Floyd was only five foot nine inches tall, and college coaches were looking for boys over six foot whose bodies would grow during weight work and eating at the training table. There was no money available for college tuition. Floyd's mother had worked hard in a sweat-shop clothing mill, and there was no savings account to allow Floyd the opportunity for undergraduate school. Three days after his high school graduation, Floyd got off a train just outside Parris Island, South Carolina. For the next thirteen weeks, he would train and become a Marine. On graduation day from recruit training, he was designated as "The Outstanding Man of Platoon 140". Another rung in the ladder had been climbed.

During the next four years, Floyd served his country, rose to the rank of Corporal, E4, picked up a few medals along the way, and found and married the love of his life, Marilyn. At the end of his enlistment, and on the advice of his commanding officer, Admiral Harry D. Felt, Commander-in-Chief of the Pacific, he matriculated at Lock Haven State University in Pennsylvania, the little Susquehanna River town where his aunt still had her business. In this new school, Floyd learned that he had another advantage---he could speak French.

As a young Marine, Floyd had been located in the central highlands of Vietnam. His job was to coordinate and work with the *Montaignards*, a highly independent group of Vietnamese who wanted no part of the Communist North. During his tour, Floyd developed a good working knowledge of the French language, and he excelled at his job, and he stayed alive. In his college French classes, Floyd drew praise from his professors, and upon graduation, he was awarded a three-year fellowship to Penn State University which would lead to a doctorate. The small-town boy from a little coal town along the Susquehanna had kept his eyes on the upper rungs of his ladder of respectability.

Floyd's training at Penn State would lead to further study at McGill University in Montreal, the University of Grenoble in France, Laval University in Quebec and a professorship at Union College in Schenectady, New York. But, before all that could take place, he had to earn a living, and he accepted a position of Foreign Language Department Head in the Saratoga Springs City Schools in upstate New York. And, there, in that school is where his students were to benefit from their teacher's desire to become the best at what he did. The games were about to begin.

CHAPTER 2

First Day Dress Blues

Floyd was about to begin his teaching career. If he knew anything, getting off on the right foot---a good start---was the key to success in his profession. Someone had told him in one of his education classes that working in front of a classroom of students was like holding a prized bird in your hand; gripping too tightly might kill the bird, too loosely might allow the bird to fly away. But, Floyd was former Marine. The way he walked, the manner of his dress from his suit and tie down to his spit-shined shoes said, "Semper Fi. I'm in control. Listen and learn with me." Floyd was ready.

In the late 60's, students were not yet addicted to either cell phones or hallucinogens. Smoking in bathrooms and at Friday-night football game parking lots made up most of the teenage infractions. Students still respected most of their teachers, and most still had respect for the pledge of allegiance to the flag. But, were these kids ready for Floyd Sarvey? Teacher orientation meetings were out of the way, and the first day of classes had arrived. Floyd was the first person at school on opening day, and he even beat the custodians to the main door, something which continued until the end of his career.

At the ringing of the bell announcing the start of the day's classes, Floyd made his way to his first class, a group of twenty-nine senior boys and girls. He stood outside his classroom door and waited for his students to arrive, take their seats and settle down. But, instead of sitting, a few late comers were still milling around, and the noise level, perhaps influenced by the nervous energy of the start of the school year, was high.

Floyd waited another thirty seconds before he entered the classroom. He then closed the door, picked up the metal waste basket and slammed it across the floor in front of his desk. Startled by what they had just experienced, the students, some still standing, suddenly became silent and openmouthed. Floyd walked to his desk, placed his leather briefcase on his desk and said, "You've got about a heartbeat to find and take a seat." Still in a trance-like state, the students went about a robotic, silent effort to find an empty seat, sat down and waited. Dr. Sarvey was about to introduce himself.

"My name is Dr. Sarvey. When addressing me, you will use that name and title. On every day, you will arrive to class on time, take your seat, place everything---books, notebooks, pens, etc., on the floor underneath your desks. If I want anything in your hands or on top of your desks, I will tell you. If for some reason you are late to class, you will have a hall pass and give it to me upon arrival. I will be your teacher of French, one of the world's most beautiful languages. You will learn to love it as do I. We will learn together. My experience with learning took place at Lock Haven University, Penn State University, McGill University in Montreal, Laval University in Quebec and the University of Grenoble in France. But, the one place where I learned the most was in Parris Island, South Carolina, the United States Marine Corps Recruit Depot. I am here with that background and education. We will have fun with French. Every Friday, we will learn a new French song. You will enjoy singing. It will improve your pronunciation, and you will be graded on your performance. Tomorrow is Friday. We will look forward to it." Dr. Sarvey had started his career.

CHAPTER 3

"Aupres de ma blonde..."

Two weeks into his first teaching year, Floyd, the new guy on the block, thought that he had made the right choice. He felt good about being in the classroom. He enjoyed working with his teenage students, and he had established a collegial working relationship with most of his fellow teachers. Oh, yes, there were some ruffled feathers among his associates. A few disgruntled foreign language educators questioned why they had been passed over for the job of department head. This new guy wasn't even brought up in the community. He hadn't paid his dues by coming up through the ranks, and just because he had a few advanced degrees, these community-bred individuals were not going to make Sarvey's job easy. For years to come, one or two grudge-holding fellow teachers did just that. Silent protests, indifference to suggested improvements and a little foot dragging did occur. It didn't bother Floyd. He had things to do.

While Floyd's students did what they were asked and followed directions to the letter, their teacher realized that the atmosphere in the classroom was too rote like. Something was needed. Yes, his students were never late to class. Their homework was completed diligently, handed in and returned, but that certain something, that *Je ne sais quoi,* was not yet in place. But, that magical moment which sometimes develops an invisible bond between student and teacher was about to materialize.

The Friday sing-a-long of French songs had been working well. Floyd's students liked the idea of ending the week on a positive note, and they realized that working together on something which would and did improve their use of the language was worth the effort. They also learned that, the better they performed, i.e., the more enthusiastically they belted out a French tune, the better their grade was at the end of a marking period. Today was Friday, and all Dr. Sarvey's students were eagerly awaiting their next song.

Floyd started his class by saying that today's song, "Aupres de ma blonde," dates back to the eighteenth century, and its tune was readily recognizable by many people throughout the world. As in all other songs, a chalk-board study took place before any vocal rendition was made. Like his other music selections, Floyd wrote out the first line of the song on the board---"*Aupres de ma blonde, il fait bon, fait bon, fait bon.*"Then, using a backward buildup translation, Floyd said, "Look at the end of the chorus. Look at *il fait bon, fait bon, fait bon.*" Then, using the principle of active participation, Floyd said, "Now, work with your neighbor and discuss this last part of the song. I'll listen as you come up with the translation." After a minute, Floyd said, "Now everyone give me an idea of what *il fait bon* means." In total full response, many students chimed in, "It's so good." Floyd said, "Super. Now, let's take a look at *ma blonde.* Do the same thing with a neighbor, and I will call on an individual for the translation." Knowing that everyone was now responsible for a possible answer, the students were animated in their effort. After less than a few seconds, Floyd called on one student, a shy young boy who seldom participated and who needed positive feedback. Without any hesitation, the boy said, "my blond girlfriend." "Pretty good", responded his teacher. "Now, alone at your desk without the help of others, look at the beginning of the song, *Aupres de,* think of prepositional phrases we have studied, and come up with the translation." Floyd waited for thirty seconds, and said, "Now, give me a volunteer for the translation of the beginning of the song."

There seemed to be some hesitation, so Floyd suggested that they review in their minds some of the prepositional phrases studied recently. Then, without planning and as if to spur on the thinking process, he walked toward his desk and inadvertently placed his hand on the edge of the desk. Thinking back to that moment, he realized his mistake, but his nonsensical placement of his hand had come about because of a need to anchor himself in place for a second. And, before he could think of what he had done, one of the more serious senior girls sitting in the rear of the class, a puzzling look on her face, raised her hand and said, "On top of?"

Everything suddenly stopped. Time itself seemed to be suspended, and an eerie silence swept over the room. Knowing that he had committed a *faux pas* of the first order, and feeling that he could not laugh out loud at his student's answer, he did the only thing possible; he held his laughter in and walked out of the room and into the hallway and then let out a burst of laughter heard throughout the school. Seconds later, Floyd returned to his classroom, stepped in front of his class, looked at the girl who had uttered, "On top of?" As calmly as possible, and without cracking a smile, Dr. Sarvey said, "No! It means alongside of or next to." And that, fellow readers is when the entire class exploded with laughter. Floyd's students finally knew that their teacher, this gruff, Marine-like man, was human. The ice which had been separating student and teacher melted immediately, and Dr. Sarvey was ready to further motivate his students.

The author's formative years

CHAPTER 4

Active Participation in the Classroom

In the early 70's, not one public school district in upstate New York had ever proposed taking students to Europe to enhance their learning. Floyd Sarvey had given the idea some thought, and he knew that such a venture would require planning and motivation. Students and parents have to believe that such a thing was possible, and that it might be worth the effort. Airport jumping off places for a trip to Europe were close. Albany transfers could place students in Boston, Montreal or New York for transatlantic flights. But first, getting students and parents interested in the study of the language, French, would require work.

Eager to start his work day, Sarvey would open his department office door every morning at 6 A.M. He and his wife now had two children, a boy and a girl, both of whom attended elementary school just blocks away from the family home. Floyd's wife, Marilyn, juggled her time at home with her work as an ophthalmic technician. She had studied for her profession, and in spite of responsibilities at home, she wholeheartedly supported her husband's determination to be as good as possible in his work. Such a willingness to lend a hand is not always forthcoming.

In the early morning hours before the first bell for classes to begin, Floyd worked on his lesson plans which included ideas on how to create interesting learning activities, projects which would enliven the learning process. He knew that if he were to inspire his students and encourage them to love what they studied, higher steps to learning might take shape. His classroom techniques had to be made of the right stuff. Learning French or any foreign language demands patience and effort. But, if one enjoys what he is doing, hard work becomes play, and play leads to a desire to continue along the path to achievement. For the next few months, new and more interesting learning activities became part of every-day lesson plans.

Until the first decade of the twentieth century, the New York State Education Department required end-of-the-year exams in each of the foreign languages taught in the public schools. Dr. Sarvey became one of the test writers of the French exam during his summers, and this exam tested all of the four skills of language learning---listening, speaking, reading and writing. In an effort to improve his students' listening comprehension, Floyd came up with an interesting activity.

Associating one of France's most popular sports, cycling, the famous *Tour de France* was brought to the attention of Floyd's students. The geographical contours of the bike race were pointed out. The different-colored T-shirts, the famous yellow jersey and national symbols worn by the riders were displayed. The twenty-something stages of the race, each stopping in a different French city, were mentioned, and a map of France was used to outline the challenging event.

As an assignment, each student was asked to cut and design a three by three inch T-shirt, and the student's name was printed on each side of the piece of clothing made out of paper. The next day, T-shirts were displayed, and a paper clip was supplied, affixed to the shirt, and hung on a line strung at the back of the classroom. On the line, at ten-inch intervals, the name of a French city was spelled out. And, at the beginning of the line, each student had placed his T-shirt which determined the starting point of the race. The first *Tour de France* in a classroom was about to begin.

At the end of each class, Dr. Sarvey's students were given a sample of a listing comprehension question and four possible answers from an old Regents exam in French. The next day, the student brought in a translation of the question and answers on a small piece of paper which included the student's name. Sarvey would then read the passage, and the students would circle what they believed to be the correct answer and pass their responses forward to the teacher. Sarvey or one of his students would determine who had answered correctly, and the T-shirts of those who had responded appropriately had their T-shirt moved to the next city on the *Tour.* Every day, upon entering Floyd's classroom, each student would immediately go to the line hanging in the rear of the classroom and confirm their standing in the race. Motivation is such a beautiful thing to behold. But, more was still to come.

In the late 70's New York State public schools no longer required students to recite the pledge of allegiance to the American flag. Yes, each classroom still displayed the Stars and Stripes, but adherence to the pledge fell by the wayside. To Floyd Sarvey, the former Marine, there was something too lax in that law. It was, at least to him, reprehensible. So, the next technique, the enhancement of speaking and pronunciation, was introduced. Floyd translated the pledge of allegiance into French. Students were assigned the memorization of the pledge, tested on their ability to write it from memory, and then tested individually on their ability to correctly recite *Je donne ma parole d'honneur au drapeau...*To this day, some of Dr. Sarvey's former students, years after graduation from high school, are not reluctant to stop him on the streets of Saratoga Springs and recite the pledge in French. That, gentle readers, makes an impression on old guys.

By the end of Floyd's third year of teaching, other learning activities, all of which involved total mental, physical and kinematic abilities, were devised and used in daily lesson plans. Hand-held chalkboards, one for each student in the class, were designed and supplied by one of Floyd's shop-teacher colleagues. On the teacher's command, various parts of the day's learning were called for, and on cue, held up for review by Dr. Sarvey. Corrections were made, and the boards erased with clean, but old socks supplied by the students. At times, a slight mist, a floating shimmer of chalk dust would loft about, and another activity would begin.

Classrooms through the 90's still contained four by eight foot slate boards attached to the front of the room. One of Floyd's activities required the students in each row, one-by-one, to run to the board and write out his person/ number depiction of a verb conjugation. Ending with the infinitive of the case, students would wait for the teacher's acknowledgement of the correct conjugation. During this "board race", students at their desk could call out and suggest changes in a student's written effort, but the noise sometimes got so loud that teachers in the upper floors of the school would stomp their feet in protest. Out of respect for his colleagues in the upper floors, a "silent running" of the conjugation race was instituted...but only when stomping from above was heard.

At the end of the board races, students would be perspiring, gasping for breath, and fortunately, none of Floyd's students ever lost consciousness. In other focusing activities, Dr. Sarvey would tell a French joke in the target language. Students would patiently listen and their comprehension would be determined when the punchline was delivered and laughter ensued. Magic tricks, French gestures and French food preparation were introduced from time to time, but the number one attention getter and motivational device was French volleyball in the classroom.

Floyd's son, Brooks, came home from elementary school one day and was having an evening meal with his family. His sister, Janine, also an elementary-school student, asked her brother what he had done in school that day. Brooks replied that he had a great day, and continued by saying, "We played volleyball in class." His father said, "You did what in the classroom?"

---Yes, Dad. Mr. McMullen strung a line across the middle of the ceiling high above our desks. He brought a nerf ball out and divided the class into two groups. We turned our chairs facing the other side of the classroom and questions were asked about what we had studied. If you raised your hand and had the right answer, you got the ball and could throw it over the cord to the students on the other side of the room. If someone caught it, they could throw it back until someone either dropped the ball or it hit the floor. That scored a point. It was so much fun!

The following week, Floyd's classroom was fitted with a string running across the middle of the classroom about eight feet off the floor. A six inch nerf ball and a reserve ball supplied by Toys-R-Us provided all that was needed, and French Volleyball in the Classroom was born. In the late 70's, Dr. Sarvey outlined his classroom activity in the Journal of the New York State Association of Foreign Language Teachers, and for his work in that area of learning, he was elected Capital District Representative of that educational group.

In the days to come, when Floyd's classes played volleyball, an activity which was used to review and reinforce learning French, his classroom door was left open. The noise, once again evidence of active participation, a mixture of laughter and applause, filtered out into the hallway, and the closing of other foreign language classroom doors could be heard. Before long, however, German, Latin and Spanish classes were happily playing their version of volleyball. You just had to be there.

CHAPTER 5

School/Community High Water Marks

Before any mention or outline of the first "April in Paris" student tours are offered (sometimes the best are saved for last), variations in language learning techniques should be made available to the reader. When Dr. Sarvey was hired as head of the public school's foreign language department, the entire foreign language staff, junior and senior high school, numbered less than seven people. When Sarvey retired in 2001, twenty-two teachers of French, Italian, Spanish and Latin made up the department staff. Such an increase in foreign language study did not come about without innovative learning techniques and motivated students.

On one winter day when the snow fall had cancelled classes for the day, Floyd still found himself in his department office. Working with his colleague, Rolland Fontaine, the two men came up with a suggestion. What if every foreign language teacher and their classes put on a display of the culture they were studying and made that display available to the community? Both agreed that the idea should be discussed in the next department meeting.

At that meeting, Floyd knew that the idea he and his colleague had discussed would be accepted by the majority of the other target language teachers. He also knew that a certain few, those still smoldering from the newcomer's arrival in their school would not immediately adopt the proposal. But, the majority prevailed. The subject of how to prepare the community, the students and their parents for such a project was brought up and discussed. The time of year for such an event was addressed, and the availability of space and exactly where the activity would be held was settled on. Floyd and his colleagues would now have to address the civil service workers, the custodians, for they, too, would play a role in the first-time adventure.

At an after-school meeting, one student representative from each of the target language classes in the school, was apprised of the upcoming event and suggested that their task was to outline the idea of a language night to their peers the next day. The student representatives were told that their individual class would offer to the public on a given night a rendition of the culture and language they were studying. The student reaction to such a project was overwhelmingly positive; students do like to have fun. The event would be called, "Foreign Language Night", and it would take place in the junior high gym, cafeteria and adjoining hallways. The first "Foreign Language Night" took place in late April when the weather had improved.

Over two thousand parents, townspeople and community members attended. The school's parking lots were full, and streets near the school were lined with automobiles. But, to fully understand the evening's event, well, you just had to be there.

That first evening, a few of the German classes offered an authentic German beer hall (root beer, that is). A Braunschweiger restaurant offered for sale smoked liver sausage and sauerkraut to hungry onlookers. The Spanish classes put together a mariachi band in full costume. Students dressed as early Spanish explorers explained to the public who they were and what they had discovered. Latin students, dressed in togas, gave talks on Roman emperors and writers. But, maybe, just maybe, the *piece de resistance* was the display put together by one of the advanced French classes. Students in this class had studied French art in preparation for their "April in Paris" trip, a subject to be discussed later. Postcards had been given out depicting famous French paintings hung and displayed in the Louvre. The students were told to work on a live display of their choice of paintings. On their own, using props borrowed from parents, friends and neighbors, live sketches were modeled by individual students.

At the entrance to the exhibit, a museum guide greeted visitors in French and in English. Live models of the *chef-d'oeuvres,* the masterpieces, stood or posed without moving for over thirty minutes while museum goers passed by and listened to tour guides explain each sketch. Short breaks were given while other visitors lined up for the tour through the Louvre.

At one station, "The Rowers", a man in 19th century garb complete with straw hat, took his lady on a glide through a cellophane lake. At another stage, a student played the French civil servant, Marat, who had been assassinated in his bath during the French Revolution. The bathtub was made from a cardboard refrigerator box. The blood, expertly displayed on the dead man's body was Heinz catsup. Napoleon, a subject painted by Jacques Louis David, proudly stood in uniform while parents and museum goers wondered whether the student playing the Emperor was himself, alive. And, beautifully dressed and sitting in place was the Mona Lisa with her magnetic smile and not moving a muscle. The Mona Lisa was portrayed by Floyd's daughter, Janine. Ah, but all good things must come to an end.

"Foreign Language Night" grew is size and in popularity for six or seven more years. Busloads of students from other schools in the area would arrive for the show and add to the growing numbers of attendees. Each year, different exhibits took place. Only two weeks of the school year were allotted to students and teachers to prepare for the one-night show. A few teachers began to complain about the work load (Floyd and some of his colleagues remained after the evening's end and helped custodians clean up the debris left over from the exhibits getting home around two A.M.) and that those two weeks were slowing down the curriculum. Bowing to the wishes of his colleagues, Floyd decided that it was time to slow down and move on to other things.

Marilyn, a reluctant portrait sitter

CHAPTER 6

Club Med Spinoffs

It took some time for Floyd to mentally cope with the fact that some of his colleagues would balk at going above and beyond that required of the classroom teacher. The very idea that a teacher would not be willing to sacrifice some unpaid time to his profession and to his students was equivalent to putting a sticky-like sludge in a finely-tuned engine; it didn't set well. For some time, the regular classroom activities continued. And, then, Floyd decided that a diversion was needed. Not for his students, but for him and his wife.

Flying from Albany to Miami and then on to Fort-de-France, Martinique was delightful. One of the Club Med stations, Martinique, was everything one could ask. Full of beautiful sights, sounds, smells and exotic beaches and clear, blue waters, the Caribbean island offered just what was needed--- a time to recharge overloaded batteries. During the day, couples from all over the world frolicked on the beach, swam in the ocean's warm water and dined on well-prepared French food. At the seaside bars set up for convenient use, colored beads were used as currency, and these were worn around the neck by visitors to the club. The G.O.'s, the *gentils organizateurs,* the club work staff, made up of young French and Americans who wanted to work a summer and enjoy the climate, were among the most accommodating personnel of any establishment. Floyd's wife, Marilyn did not know yet what the term for these people, "G.O" meant so she asked one young Frenchman. He quickly replied, "Madame, that means, "giant organ." Learning takes place quickly on the Club Med beaches.

But, it was after dinner when things really came to life. Every evening, the G.O.'s would gather near the outdoor amphitheater and call things to order. One of the *"organizateurs"* would lead the crowd in a rousing Club Med song, and then, the show would begin. Dressed in their finest clothes, the French workers would perform the latest song and dance routines of famous artists. Elvis Presley, Edith Piaf, Prince, and others would have their songs belted out over the P.A. system. But, there was a catch. Every song was in lip sync. Every effort was made to imitate the original artist. Their moves, their style, their manner of presenting a song. Comedy acts also took place, and every night, different artists were presented. Every visitor was captivated with these on-stage presentations, and all of a sudden, a new idea was born.

The next day, when Floyd could catch his fellow teacher who had a penchant for the nude beach area of the club, the two teachers discussed the possibility of whether or not such shows could be duplicated back in school. An emphatic, "Yes" was voiced by both teachers, and on the beach at Martinique, a new Saratoga Springs High School attraction was conceived. "French Night" was about to take form.

Knowing that some of his colleagues in the other target languages might still be hesitant to take on another extracurricular activity, it was agreed that only the upper levels of French, taught by Floyd and his fellow Club Med goer, would perform the first trial run of the Club Med inspired *spectacle.* As soon as they arrived back home, plans were formulated. Student representatives from the advanced French classes were informed about the new idea, and they carried back the news to their peers about an on-the-stage performance of French songs in lip sync.

Student enthusiasm for the project was instantaneous. Saratoga was known for its own Saratoga Performing Arts Center, and every student in the school had attended shows by renowned artists from all sides of the music spectrum. From rock stars to country/western to the classical, Saratoga's students had been there. Convincing them to perform on stage at school was as easy as melting chocolate on a hot summer's day. The curtain was ready to go up.

In preparation for the big evening, popular French songs, old and new, were made available. Translations of the lyrics took place. Videos, if available, were studied, and the songs were sung in class. The lyrics were memorized, and in front of the class, interested students would test their lip-syncing skills for possible selection to appear on stage. The set concerning each song was designed, and if dancing or action was required, the appropriate choreography was drawn up and practiced by the students themselves. It was show time!

In preparation for the first evening's performance of "French Night", the local newspapers carried announcements of the event. The date, time, place and description of the event were published. Special invitations were sent to the residents of local retirement centers, and parents, of course, were encouraged by their performing children to attend. The stage was set.

Saratoga's students were no strangers to hand-held microphones. They had seen them used many times at SPAC, so coming up with home-made mics was as easy as giving a baby its first pacifier. When the curtain went up for the first lip-sync presentation, students on stage were dressed in twentieth turn-of-the-century garb. Straw hats and sport coats for the boys, frilly colored dresses and parasols for the girls. In the first skit, the boy playing Maurice Chevalier strutted on stage to a tune about the Queen of England and lip-synced the lyrics in French perfectly to the tune coming from a P.A. system supplied by the school's music department. In the background, other early twentieth-century characters mimed the actions of the story sung by Chevalier. The audience howled their approval, and they were still applauding when the curtain went down so the second act could get ready.

In the second scene, Josephine Baker, the black American expatriate from Saint Louis who moved to Paris and lived out her life as a cabaret singer belted out *"J'ai deux amours..."*. The curtain went down after each song, and in the interim, the stage was reset for the next performance. While that took place, a student was out in front of the curtain announcing in French and in English what was to take place next. By the third song, Floyd, his colleague, and the other target language teachers in attendance knew that "French Night" had taken off, and was to be an annual event. Crowds at these performances rivaled those which took place for school concerts, and at several lip-sync events, standing room only was the case. Some of the on-stage presentations were unforgettable. Floyd's grandson, Mackinley, did such a good rendition of Charles Trenet's *La Mer* that he received a standing ovation at the end. Complete in tux and white gloves, Mack even had a lip tremor when Trenet's high notes were hit.

Weeks after the first "French Night", Floyd's Spanish-teaching colleagues questioned why just French was chosen for such a night. Floyd's answer was a simple, "Well, I guess you just had to be there."

CHAPTER 7

Allons-y! Let's go to Paris!

In 1973, Floyd decided to initiate plans for the first "April in Paris" school-sponsored trip to Europe. Little did he know that his school administrators and the Board of Education might have questions about such a proposal. His superintendent said, "You're going to take over forty students to France for ten days? Can you imagine the financial responsibility for such an undertaking?' Those were just some of the protestations voiced by the administration. But, the one statement which proved to be golden was, "You realize, Dr. Sarvey, that the Board of Education will have to set some rules concerning who should and should not go, how these students will be chaperoned, and whether school time can be allotted for the trip." That's all it took. Floyd's students would go to Paris, but it would be he who set the rules, and no school time would be asked for.

Knowing that a school recess took place in April, and that ten days would be allotted for that vacation from classes, plans were drawn up a year in advance of the first trip. In the month of May at the end of the school year before closing for the summer, sophomores and juniors enrolled in advanced French classes were told that in the following year, in April, the opportunity to travel to Paris would come up. If interested, the students could discuss the trip over the summer and perhaps find a part-time job toward saving for the cost.

In Saratoga, summer employment opportunities abound for students looking for part-time work. The Saratoga Performing Arts Center and the Saratoga Flat Track, the premiere race track for thoroughbreds in the United States, hire hundreds of students for summer work. Restaurants, bulging with visitors attending those two venues would seek good food and service. Saratoga's students of French all of a sudden became wage earners.

Tour companies which catered to youth groups traveling to Europe were contacted. Bus companies which offered round-trip connections to nearby airports gave information on cost and availability. The meeting room of the local library was booked for one Sunday evening per month for the entire year. That was important because that was where rules and regulations concerning the trip would be discussed and made clear with students and parent/guardians. No school premises would be used, and no school time would be lost. After all, the upcoming April recess was ten days long. And, large groups would not be a problem for Dr. Sarvey. As a young Marine, he had crossed the Pacific three times with twenty-five hundred other jarheads on navy troop ships. Forty or fifty students, parents and guardians would not be a problem on a transatlantic flight.

In September, at the start of the new school year, the first meeting of the "April in Paris" trip took place at the public library. Over one hundred students, parents and guardians attended the Sunday night meeting, and they listened, took notes and asked questions. The entire tour on a day-by-day basis was outlined. Exact dates, time of departure, return times and the names of teacher chaperones were presented. And, yes, the price for the trip was given. For less than $800.00, all meals with the exception of lunch (students would be advised how to seek out and order in French their own lunch), all transfers to and from airports, all hotel accommodations and tips (*pourboires)* for the French tour guides were included. Since that first trip, prices have risen, but in the mid 70's, the economy was conducive to air travel to Europe.

During the first meeting, it was further explained that the once-a-month Sunday night meetings would be mandatory. No exceptions would be made, although, in emergency situations, members of the immediate family could sit in, take notes and be responsible for imparting knowledge to the absentee gained at the meeting. Not one student missed a meeting that year. Applications were handed out to all in attendance, and a deadline for their return with a first installment of $200.00 was stated. The deadline called for those wishing to make the trip to return their completed applications and down payment to be handed in at school by the end of September. Parents and guardians were told that they, too, could make the trip contingent upon space available in a "students first" quota.

On the first day back at school after the meeting, forty-five applications complete with deposits were handed in. "April in Paris" was a go. Each month, a different subject was covered. In October, applications for passports and their due date for completion were distributed. Travelers would be required to show their passports at future meetings. In November, the French currency, then the French *franc*, was shown and its value in comparison to the American dollar explained. In December, the *voyageurs* were told exactly what to take along on the trip in the way of clothing, cameras, hair dryers, basic needs and, of course, what not to bring. Dr. Sarvey told the group, "Lay out everything you think necessary to make the trip on your bed at home. Then, step back and cut that amount of things in half and put that in one suitcase. If you bring two suitcases, one will be left behind when we board the bus for the airport." No one had more that none suitcase.

As the meetings continued and the month of April drew near, the Paris metro system was explained, studied and tested. Using an authentic four by five foot map of the metro, the students were given a destination on the map and, in front of their peers and parents, an imaginary trip was taken. Metro riders pointed out their route on the map using yard sticks. Cuisine was explained, and how to order a French baguette, cheese and potted meat for a cheap afternoon snack was offered up. Having to order one's own lunch in the language made for attention-getting instruction.

Parental consent forms allowing their children to have or not to have the right to order a small glass of wine at the evening meal were circulated. At the time, the drinking age in France was fifteen. Every parent/guardian signed the permission slips in the affirmative. April had arrived. Time to pack.

Mr. Fontaine on right. The blue comb's finder on left

CHAPTER 8

The Origin of the "Walking Dead"

Departure day had arrived. Very early in the morning, student and adult travelers, chaperones, parent/guardians and grandparents were waiting in front of the senior high school for their bus to JFK. Goodbyes were said, and the bus loaded the group for New York City. The atmosphere on the bus was action packed.

Some of the travelers on the bus had never been on an airplane, and the electricity from nervous anticipation, if bottled, could have powered the lights of Saratoga for an entire year. New student relationships took place quickly. Teacher chaperones and other adults, all sitting in the front of the bus, got a chance to know each other better in a matter of minutes. In the two and a half-hour ride to the airport, there was a constant chatter throughout the bus. Before anyone knew it, the bus was pulling up to the terminal at JFK.

The tour group had been informed that everyone would stay together in the departing plane area once bags were checked. That completed, a designated spot where everyone would assemble one half hour before boarding was pointed out. Last minute snacks were purchased and Floyd, his wife, Marilyn, and the other adults settled in and waited for the call to board. When that call came, the entire group of fifty Saratogians made its way to the designated seating area on an Air France jet.

Floyd made sure that the entire group had a spot near the rear of the aircraft. Once seated, the group was told that a meal would be served during the flight, and that upon landing the next morning, everyone was to remain seated until other travelers had gotten their belongings and left the cabin. No one was to leave the plane before their chaperones led them to the plane's exit.

At 8 P.M., the transatlantic Air France jet rolled down the runway and they were off. The Saratoga group had been awake since 5 A.M. that morning, and the nervous energy had not yet dissipated. Not one of the group slept during the six and a half-hour flight across the Atlantic. Everyone talked about what would be seen once in France. Last minute checks of equipment, currency, passports and cameras were made. At 8 A.M., Paris time the next morning, the plane was approaching the city of Paris and headed toward Charles De Gaulle Airport. One of the students who had been looking out a window said, "I can see the Eiffel Tower". The plane was coming in for a landing.

Floyd asked his wife, Marilyn, to look out the window and get a view of the famous French landmark. Unfortunately, the only thing Mrs. Sarvey saw was the inside of a paper bag. Some people were still affected by the plane's motion while in the air. Marilyn was no exception.

Upon landing and while the plane was still taxing to its assigned dock, Floyd announced to his group that no one was to move or get out of their seats until the rest of the other passengers had departed the cabin. The Air France flight attendants, all smartly dressed young women, became nervous when the group of fifty Americans were still seated as others left the cabin. Dr. Sarvey called for a show of passports, and everyone responded by holding their official documents high above their heads. That confirmed, he said, "Make sure you have all your belongings, and follow me off the plane. Do not lose sight of the person in front of you, and stick together at all times until we get through customs. From there, we will board the bus for Paris". Then, in a Marine-like command, he said, "Saratoga up!" Like jack-in-the-box puppets, the entire group rose as one unit and followed their leader and Mr. Fontaine down the aisle and off the plane.

Sheep-like, the Saratoga group filed through customs and waited in an orderly pack just outside the Charles De Gaulle terminal. A French tour guide greeted the group and conducted it to an awaiting bus. Once on board, introductions were made, and the "April in Paris" tour was headed into the city and to their hotel. That's when it hit. Sleep deprivation, a tactic used in the torture of others, invaded the bus, and as if to cast an eye-closing spell, the tour guide began her P.A. system explanation of the history of sights zipping by just outside the bus windows.

Floyd looked back through the bus at his flock, now comfortably seated and relaxed to the point of total withdrawal. The stress had been lifted like a giant weight taken off their shoulders. He looked at Marilyn and said, "Oh, my God. We've been gassed!" The entire group, students and adults, looked like the cast of a movie from the "Walking Dead". Heads laid back, mouths open wide exposing tongues, drool and chewing gum, eyes rolled back exposing only the whites, it was a sight not to be forgotten. Staying awake for over thirty hours had taken its toll. Floyd's fellow chaperone, Mr. Fontaine, said, "Do you think any of them are still alive?" It was a sight to behold, but...yep, you had to be there.

CHAPTER 9

The Hotel Dagmar and the Privy

Oblivious to the drone of the tour guide's verbal review of the history of Paris and its monuments, Floyd's bus load of first-time visitors to Paris were dead to the world. Their chaperone decided to let them get a little rest. They had a big day ahead. Knowing that the chances of booking rooms at the George V or the Ritz were few and none, Floyd wondered what was in store for him at the Dagmar Hotel. All everyone needed was a base of operations and a place to get a good night's rest. Before long, the bus pulled up to the hotel's entrance.

The hotel had seen its best days in the *Belle Epoque*, the last quarter of the nineteenth century. The building was three stories high and showed some neglect. Yet the entrance way was colorful and welcoming in a rustic sort of way. And, not a lot of time is spent in a hotel by tourists. The tour guide ushered in her passengers, now fully awake and carrying their suitcases. Room assignments were made; three to four to a room for students, two or three to a room for adults and married couples.

Dr. Sarvey and his co-chaperone were given a master list of room numbers and the names of occupants, and everyone was told to meet in the hotel lobby in one hour. The chaperones waited behind in the lobby to answer questions from the group if any problems arose. Not too much time passed before the questions came. "Dr. Sarvey, we don't have a shower in our room, and we were told that there was one washroom per floor where we could clean up." Yep, the group was not at the Ritz, but everyone was told that by overcoming little problems and sticking together, things would turn out alright. Both students and adults were resilient in their effort to remain positive; Floyd had a strong contingent of fellow travelers.

Because of the lack of up-to-date bathroom facilities, the one-hour time limit for the group meeting was extended. Lines formed in front of restroom areas, and before too long, the group was ready to take on the day. Once collected into a unit and out of the way of other hotel guests, the fifty Americans made their way through the Latin Quarter, a spot where French university students gathered and found good-quality restaurants for a modest price. Window shopping took place immediately and at special intervals, several orientation points were pointed out to the group so that, on free days, everyone could find their way back to the hotel. After that orientation walk, the orderly mob made its way back to the Hotel Dagmar for dinner and a good night's rest.

At the evening meal served on the hotel's ground floor at 7 P.M., everyone was hungry and wondered what might be served. In spite of the

Allen R. Remaley

hotel's lack of the finer things, the meal proved
to be just what was needed. The hotel's chefs
understood American eating habits. That first
evening meal included hamburgers on a bun,
French fries, fresh vegetables, and apple pie and
ice cream for dessert. Everyone was suddenly
recharged and waiting for an announcement
concerning the next day's activity. During the
meal, students tried out their target language
on the French servers. One American, a good-
looking girl, was asked if she would like
seconds. She proudly announced, *"Non, merci,
monsieur, je suis pleine."* The young French
waiter laughed out loud and responded, *"Mais,
mademoiselle, Felicitaitions! C'est formidable."*
Not knowing that the French word, *"pleine",*
had two meanings; one, "full", and the other,
"pregnant", the American French student soon
found out that she had been congratulated on
her recent development. That story circulated
quickly among the dinner party, and it was now
time for bed checks for the "April in Paris" group.

Adults were left on their own and told about
the times for the next morning's departure. Floyd
and Mr. Fontaine, made their rounds of every
student room, confirmed occupancy and head
counts, and told the students that taped across
the door sill of every room was a piece of masking
tape with the chaperones' initials written on
the tape. Only on emergencies were students
to open their doors, and if the tape was found
disturbed the next morning, tough questioning
would take place. Thinking everything secure,
the chaperones, now tired from shepherding
fifty people through their first day in Paris, went
to bed. Ah, the false pretenses of such people.

Around 1 A.M., Floyd heard a knock at his bedroom door. When he opened it, there stood one of his female senior-citizen travelers with a look of consternation on her face. "Dr. Sarvey, I have to go to the bathroom, and someone else has been in there for over an hour. I know it's the same person, because I can hear them saying something to me in French when I knock."

Wanting to relieve the mental stress as well as the physical discomfort of his adult traveler, Floyd asked the woman to show him the way to *Les toilettes* at the end of the hall. She did just that stopping in front of a door with a sign in big letters printed across front which said, *PRIVE*. Floyd ask the woman what she thought that word said. She replied, "It means 'privy', we had one of those back home when I was growing up." Without even cracking a smile, the doctor said, "Mary, that word means, 'private', and it's the maid's room. I have an idea what she was saying to you when you knocked on her door. I will tell you what she said tomorrow." With that, the kind lady was escorted to the door which said, "*Toilettes*" and "WC". All good things come to an end.

Janine and Brook's first trip

CHAPTER 10

Boys and Girls at the Dagmar Hotel

At this first trial run of the "April in Paris" Saratoga tours, Floyd had somehow forgotten that raging hormones held sway over the minds and bodies of teenagers. Caught up in the day-to-day, hour-to-hour problem-solving grind, the stress of making sure of the safety of his group and determining whether or not his entourage got what they had paid for, sexual attraction of the opposites in foreign lands had escaped him for the moment. Things do change fast.

During the next few days, the Saratoga fifty visited Versailles and its famous Hall of Mirrors. Near the seventeenth-century chateau, students and adults also had a chance to visit *Le Hameau,* Marie Antoinette's miniature farm where she shepherded her pet sheep which had been painted in various colors. After the visit to the chateau and its grounds, the bus took the group back to Paris where a visit to the Louvre, the world's largest museum, took place. There, museum goers were treated to paintings by French and Italian masters, and, of course, gazed at the Mona Lisa, Leonardo de Vinci's masterpiece. Everyone was astonished that the famous painting was so small in comparison to others hanging on the museum walls.

A one-time visit to the Louvre, formerly the royal palace before Louis XIV built Versailles, will not suffice. Floyd had been there several times before, and he had yet to see only half of what was kept in that magnificent place. In the afternoon after lunch in the Latin Quarter, the entire contingent took a ride on the metro and got off at the Champ de Mars exit. At that stop, a vast park opened up which led to the entrance to *Les Invalides,* once a hospital for the soldiers of Louis XIV and now the burial place of Napoleon I. The Champ de Mars is a large grassy, one-hundred yard long park, and it had to be crossed to get to the building which housed Napoleon's tomb. So, in keeping with military tradition, Floyd told his platoon of tourists that they would march into the building area. After all, the gates leading into the monument housing the tomb were guarded by soldiers from the French Army. Marching seemed appropriate.

Floyd and his fellow chaperones had the group form columns of three. The marchers were given a quick lesson on cadence steps and marching count and told that they would repeat in unison the lines of a famous Marine Corps marching song. The now military-inspired group repeated and belted out each line of the song as they covered the ground...

I don't want no teenage queen,
I just want my M14,

If I die in the combat zone,
Pack me up and ship me home,
Pin my medals upon my chest,
Tell my momma I did my best,
Bury me deep in the sand and clay,
When I hit the bottom you'll hear me say,
I wanna be a drill instructor,
I wanna cut off all my hair,
I wanna be a drill instructor,
I wanna wear a Smokey Bear,
Your Corps,
Our Corps,
My Corps,
Marine Corps,
Hou-Rah!

A platoon of Marine recruits could not have done better. In a loud and clear unified chant, the group moved across the Champ de Mars with military precision. The gate guards watched in amazement as the unit approached them at the entrance to the monument. Open mouthed and staring at the oncoming mass of fifty people, the guards must have wondered whether to run or open fire. They did neither, and as the marching wonders passed the guards, Floyd fired a smart salute to each one of the defenders of the gate.

No adequate description of Napoleon's Tomb can be documented on paper. The majesty and size of the sarcophagus is just too impressive to portray in words. Red Corsican marble, magnificent in dimension, the final resting place of the Emperor just has to be witnessed on site. Well, you just have to be there.

After the afternoon's visit to *Les Invalides,* the group made its way back to the hotel and prepared for dinner. At that evening meal, many stories would be told and embellished about what had been seen, done and sung during the day. Everyone was soon ready for a good night's rest...or so Floyd thought until later that night.

Earlier that same afternoon, another tour group had arrived at the Dagmar for a two-night's stay. About ten or fifteen Italian teenage boys and their chaperone had checked in and were in the hotel's hallways as Floyd's students made their way back to their rooms and got ready for bed checks. With that chore finished, Floyd and the rest of the adults retired for the night.

Around midnight, Floyd heard a knock at his door. It turned out to be the same senior citizen who had the problem with the privy, and he immediately began to question whether there might be a slight hint of Alzheimer's disease. But, the woman spoke up and said, "Dr. Sarvey, you should check the room opposite ours. There's some noise going on in there." Floyd assured the woman that he would check immediately, and he did just that.

A few of the Italian boys were sitting on the stairway steps just outside the girls' room. While Floyd's Italian was not perfect, and thinking that the boys had studied French, he used that language and told the boys that it would be best if they moved along. Comprehension took place immediately and the young men did as they were asked. Floyd then knocked on the door where four of his girls were sharing a room. The door opened a crack and standing just inside the room was one of his students dressed in what Floyd thought was the top half of a Herold's of Hollywood teddy. He dared not

45

confirm what he was thinking and kept his eyes high above the girl's head and said, "Get some clothes on. I'm coming in." The young maiden replied, "Oh, Dr. Sarvey. Everything is OK. Some boys were bothering us earlier. It's OK, now." Sarvey repeated, "Step back, get some clothes on. I'm coming in."

Seconds later, Floyd was in the room, snapped on the bedroom lights and confirmed that two of the room's female occupants were in bed. Two others, now fully dressed were cowering next to a wall on the left side of the bed. Off to Floyd's right, a curtain had been strung up offering privacy to a toilet area. When the sound of a bottle dropping on the floor behind that curtain took place, Floyd lifted a part of the material and looked at two Italian boys, one bent over the other and eyes tightly shut mimicking small animals which sometimes use such a ruse to confuse predators; if I don't see you, you don't see me. Floyd had to act.

Once again, thinking that the boys knew some French, Floyd, using a soft but emphatic voice of authority, said, "*Si vous comprenez le francais, inclinez la tete*"Without opening their eyes, the boys nodded their heads indicating that they understood the language. Then, Floyd told the two blind young men, "*Si vous bougez or si vous changez de position, vous allez mourir. Je peux facilement vous tuer comme de petits chiens. Inclinez la tete si vous me comprenez.*" Once again, head nodding indicated that the boys had gotten the message that, if they moved or changed position, they would die like little dogs.

Once an understanding had settled in, Floyd turned to his American girls and instructed them, "Get dressed, pack your bags and take them to Mrs. Sarvey's room." Without a word, the girls began to follow instructions. Mr. Fontaine had arrived on the scene by this time, and Floyd asked him to locate the Italian chaperone and bring him to the girls' room. Pulling back the bed sheet which had acted as a temporary curtain shielding the two Italian boys, Floyd confirmed that they were still frozen in place as had been instructed. For the reader to discover the result of this unfolding story, you either had to be there or continue reading the next chapter.

CHAPTER 11

The Good, the Bad and the Ugly

In thirty-seven years of classroom teaching, Floyd Sarvey had never once touched, let alone struck, any of his students, boy or girl. Yes, he had broken up school-hallway fights, but no physical violence ever took place on his part. Whether he would extend that courtesy to the Italian boys was now in question. But, within minutes, the Italian chaperone arrived on scene.

Floyd introduced himself, shook hands with his Italian equivalent, explained the situation, and pulled back the improvised curtain to expose the now statue-like boys still in place, one bending over the other with eyes closed. A torrent of Italian curses flew from the Italian educator's mouth. He yelled and screamed what Floyd believed to be threats of spending time in Dante's *Inferno*, and then he quickly moved in and grabbed each boy by the neck. He stood them up and slapped them both across the face several times. The boys, now teary-eyed with heads bowed in shame remained silent. The chaperone turned to Floyd and said, "Monsieur, Ca vous va?" Floyd assured his counterpart that what he had done was more than sufficient, and the boys were dragged out of the room and into their own sleeping area. It was now time for Floyd and his co-chaperone to attend to their own business with the four girls.

Doing as they had been told, the four girls had carried their packed luggage and were waiting in Floyd's room with Mrs. Sarvey. When they arrived, Floyd and Mr. Fontaine instructed the girls to write their names and home phone numbers on a piece of paper. While they did that, Floyd picked up the room's phone as if to make a call. Making sure that there was no dial tone, he spoke to an imaginary operator and asked that he be connected to the Air France reservation desk. He waited the appropriate amount of time, orally booked reservations for four teenage girls with a ghost representative and hung up the phone's receiver.

Pandemonium struck immediately, and it was a terrible thing to see. As if manipulated by a puppeteer's strings, the girls went to their knees and pleaded for mercy. Tears flowed like fountains, noses filled with mucus (Mrs. Sarvey supplied the girls with tissues) and supplications and promises of full religious living ensued. Floyd, in his infinite wisdom, decided that the girls had been punished enough. But, he wasn't entirely through. He began by saying, "I want you to listen, and I want you to listen well. You will not speak. The only reason I am not calling your parents and having them meet you at JFK is because they have already sacrificed by giving you a chance of a lifetime. They sent you to Paris." He continued with, "From this moment on, all of you will be responsible for wake up calls for the entire Saratoga contingent, students and adults. You will make sure that everyone has breakfast and when that is complete, you will report to me that everyone is ready for the morning's activity. Is that understood?" A nod of the heads and wiping of eyes and noses took place, but it did not suffice. Floyd repeated, "Is that understood? And this time, I want a verbal answer." In unison, the girls uttered, "Yes, Monsieur." Floyd replied, "Well, at least half your answer was in French. Now, go back to your room, but keep your bags packed. If I cannot get your reservations cancelled, I will knock on your door."

The girls slinked back to their room and left Floyd, his wife and Mr. Fontaine alone. As soon as the three chaperones were sure that the girls had made it to their room, the adults stifled any built-up laughter. Then, the adults looked at each other and Floyd said, "What if I had gotten a dial tone?" That's when the dam broke and laughter flowed.

As harsh as it might have been, one thing was sure---for the rest of the trip, the chaperones would not have to worry about wakeup calls. To this day, other than the documentation of the errant ways of some Italian boys and American girls, not one word of that evening's event has ever been divulged to anyone. One of the girls is now a Saratoga business woman. Another is following her family's tradition of practicing law. All four are mothers whose children might someday take a trip to Paris. But, being there was half the fun.

Janine – "Monsieur l'agent, le nom du soldat inconnu, s'il vous plaît?"

CHAPTER 12

The Latin Quarter and the Metaphysical Transformation of Sister Kathleen

Before any adventures of further "April in Paris" happenings can be divulged to the reader, the first launch of 1973, still had a few eye openers. The Italian group had departed from the Hotel Dagmar, and the Saratoga contingent was more than halfway through their stay in the City of Light. Students and adults had mastered the art of ordering their favorite pastries from *Les Patisseries* which were found on almost every block in the city, and they were proud of their use of the target language to command a *religieuse*, the caramel or chocolate-filled three-tiered cream puff which looked like and was called, in French, "a nun".

The Americans learned that the Latin Quarter, the famous area frequented by French university students, was a great place to have lunch and not pay too much in doing so. The students had been advised to stick together in small clusters of three to four. By walking through the quarter, Floyd ran across little gatherings of his students sitting in open-air restaurants and blending in with others their own age. Such things make teachers happy.

On their free days, students and adults could choose whether they wanted to revisit the Louvre, Napoleon's Tomb, Notre Dame Cathedral, window shop for souvenirs or have their portraits done in Montmartre at the *Place du Tertre*, a veritable tourist trap animated by cafes, restaurants, art-galleries, the bustle of street artists offering up their sometimes first-rate canvases or a charcoal portrait of a client. Many of the students and some adults found that sitting for a portrait done by one of the local French artists would supply a great souvenir and present to take home for parents. Knowing that such a thing would please both the sitting subject and their parents, Floyd took these souvenir seekers to the little square of Montmartre and gave some advice on how to barter and choose an artist.

As they were approaching the *Place du Tertre*, the little artists' square, Floyd told his flock that they should first walk around the area and watch some artists do their work. His entourage was told to look carefully at the person whose portrait was being drawn and then, when the picture was finished, compare the finished product with the sitter. If a good rendition of the person who posed resulted, it was then that you should approach the artist and inquire about the price. Doing so, especially on a pleasant April afternoon was one of the highlights of the trip. And it was there in this little square that Floyd discovered Mark, one of the better artists.

Doing exactly what he had asked his students to do---walk around and investigate the completed sketches---, Floyd came across the work of one young artist who was capturing an excellent likeness of his subjects. When the artist had finished with one of his paintings, Floyd walked up, introduced himself in French and asked if he could do one more portrait before he left for the day. The artist agreed and asked that Floyd take a seat in front of him. Floyd quickly explained that he would not be the subject of the portrait, but that it would be his wife, Marilyn. Floyd wanted this to be the one souvenir he would hold dear for the rest of his life, and he called Marilyn over to where Mark, the artist, was getting ready for his next portrait. But, there was a problem.

Back home in New York during the planning of the tour, Floyd's wife was more than hesitant to commit to accompanying her husband on this first trip. She and her husband had two small children, and at the time, there was no way that the two could accompany their parents on such an adventure. Floyd had suggested that his mother and his grandmother, both of whom were still living, would jump at the chance of having their grandchildren for ten days. With some reservation, Marilyn accepted the proposal and decided to go to Paris with her husband.

Floyd had explained all this to his artist, Mark, who during the explanation, had divulged that he was a French engineer working in Brazil.

On his holidays, he would return to France and practice his skill as an artist in Montmartre. He then turned his attention to Mrs. Sarvey, his model, and began to sketch. In that portrait in charcoal on paper, Mark captured the reluctance of a young mother who was sacrificing her time away from her children. That portrait, still cherished by Floyd as one of the most beautiful souvenirs he ever had, hangs in the family home in Saratoga Springs. After the artist and his model said their goodbyes, it was time to head back to the Latin Quarter.

While organizing the trip to Paris, a representative from the Catholic High School in town caught word of the project and made a phone call asking if she and her six students might be part of the travel party. Wanting to keep the community's good will, Floyd instructed the caller and her students to make the first meeting in September and decide for themselves whether or not to make the trip. They did just that.

Picture a young woman in her mid-twenties. No makeup, plainly dressed in a dark wool skirt, sweater, a nun's headdress and glasses. Her footwear resembled Jump Boots. But, her smile was genuine, and she was happy to have been included among those interested in traveling. Sister Kathleen and her following did not miss a meeting, and it is suffice to know that what takes place in Paris does not always remain there.

That day at the artists' quarter had ended, and portrait sitters with souvenirs under arm made their way back to the Latin Quarter for some last-minute purchases of the *religieuses*, those precious little delicious nun-like looking pastries. Floyd and his wife, Marilyn, portrait in hand, stepped off the metro at the Boulevard St. Michel station, and they started making their way along that famous street. Floyd had already had too many sugary nuns during his stay in the city, and he was not quite ready for the surprise walking toward him.

Both Floyd and his wife stopped and stared up the street. They had just noticed a beautiful young woman walking toward them. Marilyn said to her husband, "Floyd, Isn't that...?" Approaching them was a curvaceous, long-haired beauty, now wearing something which resembled a Giorgio Armani dress, high heels and carefully-applied lipstick and makeup. She strode like a runway model at a Kardashian clothing show, and she knew full well that she was the point of fixation of everyone on the boulevard, especially the young French university students on the corners. She seemed to be bathing in this new-found magnetism, and the sway of her hips made waves in the eyes of the young Frenchmen along her path. Floyd said to his wife, "Yes, Hon, that's...or used to be Sister Kathleen."

Floyd and his wife greeted this miraculous transformation by saying, "Why, Sister Kathleen, what a nice outfit!" The woman in front to them replied, "Yes, I've been shopping. Do you like it?"

---Perfect. Will we see you later?

---Well, I've been asked out for dinner. I'll be back for bed check though.

---No problem. We'll see you this evening.

---OK, bye-bye.

Three days after arriving back in New York, Sister Kathleen left the sisterhood and applied for a teaching position in an area public school. The chances are good that she is now married and the mother of small children. Sister Kathleen did not make it back to the hotel for room checks. Paris does sometime cast a magic spell.

CHAPTER 13

Touching Every Base Before Home

The last few days before the trip back to New York had arrived. Saratoga's first "April in Paris" tour was coming to an end, and Floyd wanted to make sure his students and fellow travelers would be able to talk about their experience and the highlights of Paris. While they had discovered the treasures of the Louvre, had their souvenir portraits done in Montmartre, walked through the Hall of Mirrors in Versailles, admired the outside and the interior of Notre Dame Cathedral, and contemplated the Tomb of Napoleon, there were still a few stops worth making before the flight home. Among these was a visit to the icon of all monuments---The Eiffel Tower.

In his university days studying in Paris, Floyd had learned a little trick when taking visitors to see the giant monument in steel. Getting there at the exact moment of the day was important, and Floyd knew that Gustave Eiffel's 1889 creation was worth seeing at the right time. Dr.

Sarvey collected his fifty travelers and boarded a metro car headed for the opposite side of the Seine River directly across from the tower.

Keeping his group intact, everyone left the metro car once they had reached the stop just outside President Wilson Boulevard. That exit allowed entrance to the *Palais de Chaillot* and its magnificent terrace from which a great view of the Eiffel Tower could take place. But, this evening, instead of the monument being bathed in light, it was totally dark. For the Saratoga tourists, the darkened tower was an anticlimax...a good thing. Sarvey brought the group together in a circle and told them, "Tonight, the Mayor of Paris has a special treat for us. Look across the river at the monument. Keep your eyes on it. Wait! Wait!" At that very moment, a thousand lights illuminated the majestic structure in all its splendor. From the center of the circle of admirers came an appreciative, "Ooh! Ooh! Look at that!" Pure amazement and joy erupted, and that said it all. One student said, "Dr. Sarvey, did you do that for us?"

---Of course, I do that every night at seven o'clock.

The walk across the Iena Bridge leads directly over the Seine and to the entrance way of the Eiffel Tower. The walk took little time since everyone was eager to climb the monument. Before long, tickets to the elevators leading to the second stage of the tower were handed out, and all were transported to the second level, the best spot for seeing the City of Lights in all its majesty. In the distance, Notre Dame Cathedral, now well lighted, could be made out. The Louvre, the Arch of Triumph and Montmartre glowed as if powered by some giant electric engine. The *bateaux mouches,* tourist excursion boats, plied the Seine like some enormous water bugs crossing a silvery stream. It was a sight like no other.

The whole band of city gazers stayed on the tower for some time. Sarvey and Mr. Fontaine told the group that they were free to stay on the tower and take pictures and that bed check was extended until 11:30 P.M. That announcement brought on another, "Ooh!" One day left in town, but there was more to do.

The following day, Floyd took his now well-informed tourists to the Pantheon, France's Temple of Fame located in the Latin Quarter. Once a Christian church, the edifice had been converted to house the bodies of famous French men and women. The tombs of Voltaire, Rousseau, Hugo, Louis Braille, Zola and Pierre and Marie Curie were pointed out. But, Sarvey's visitors were not any longer interested in the authors of *The Hunchback of Notre Dame, Candide,* the inventor of the system of writing for the blind or the discovers of radium. What they wanted was to encounter another pastry shop and purchase a *religieuse.* Knowing that, their leader moved the group to an unknown part of the Latin Quarter.

In 52 B.C., Julius Cesar brought his Roman Army to Paris and renamed the city, Lutece. During the next two hundred years, a Roman city was built on the square where Notre Dame Cathedral is located, and Romans required an arena. The remains of that arena still exist, and students were walked through that area on their way to more important things---*Les Patisseries.*

After dinner that evening, the troop made its way to the *Arc de Triomphe,* the massive arch commemorating Napoleon's famous battles. Commissioned in 1800, the arch was not completed during Napoleon's lifetime, but served as a place where his body lay in state before his burial in *Les Invalides.* Besides being an exhibit of famous sculptures commemorating the history of France, the arch is now also known as the burial place of the French Unknown Soldier killed in WWI. Floyd wanted that sacred place to be seen.

The entire contingent of Saratogians were escorted via metro to the stopping off place at Place Charles de Gaulle. Getting to the arch on foot is almost impossible by walking since the twelve avenues radiating from the center make one huge traffic circle. Using an underpass running from the Champs Elysees to the Arch of Triumph is better; it saves precious lives. And, the large tourist group was led through the tunnel to the center of the arch. Once in place, the students marveled at the size of the monument, and they were mesmerized with the eternal flame at its base. That was the spot reserved for the Tomb of the Unknown French Soldier.

At that point, Floyd called his students together and asked for a volunteer who would be brave enough to use the target language and ask a question of the *gendarme*, a soldier of the French Army guarding the tomb. One brave person, a girl, stepped up and was ready for the mission. Sarvey gave her the assignment. Using her target language, she was charged with asking the French soldier on duty what the name was of the soldier buried in the tomb. She understood her orders, and without hesitation, approached the young man on duty. Everyone else watched in silence hoping to discover the name of the occupant in the grave. They watched. The girl did her best using a reasonable version of the French language. Unexpectedly, the soldier being questioned threw his arms up in the air in exasperation exclaiming, "Mais, mademoiselle, c'est un soldat inconnu! Il n'a pas de nom!"

The heroic volunteer returned to her circle of friends and gave the information saying, "The soldier said that he doesn't have a name." Once the ruse was fully understood by everyone, the girl's friends laughed and hugged their heroine. She had performed her duty. Floyd apologized to his volunteer, and he knew that, if any future trips were to take place, the name of the unknown soldier would be sought out by others proud of their knowledge of the target language. It was now time to take his heroic group home.

Janine's transformation portrait

CHAPTER 14

Saratoga Trunk

It was time to pack. Souvenirs, cameras, passports and take-home presents for parents and family were carefully accounted for and placed in suitcases for safekeeping. The bus ride to Charles De Gaulle Airport became animated. Floyd's tourists were calling out the names of monuments and familiar landmarks visited during their stay in Paris, and before long, the bus pulled into the air terminal just north of the city. Head checks were made, passports reviewed, and the group made its way inside and headed for the gate from which boarding would take place. One hour later, the big Air France jet rolled down the runway, soared into the air and headed west toward the United States.

The transatlantic flight home was quiet. The sightseers were tired. They had gone all out in their quest to experience the City of Light, and they deserved a good rest. Ahead of them, once they landed in New York, they had a three-hour bus ride north to Saratoga. Sarvey knew that rest was needed by all in his group, but until all his students and the other adults on the bus were safely in the school's parking lot, he himself could not close his eyes.

During the flight, meals and snacks were served. Around noon, Eastern Standard Time, the big French jet landed at JFK. Once again, as a unit, Floyd's contingent remained seated until the other passengers had departed the plane's cabin. Then, on his command, everyone rose and left the plane together and headed for customs. A bus was waiting, the group boarded, head checks were made once more, and the bus headed toward Route 87 and the Northway to Saratoga.

The bus ride north was no longer quieted by worn-out travelers. Everyone looked out the bus windows and were happy to see that leftover winter snows had melted, and buds on trees were peeping out. The nervous expectation of having completed the trip of a lifetime was on everyone's lips, and teenagers were eager to relate to their parents the marvels they had witnessed. A happy mood swept through the bus, and in less than three hours, the group was pulling in to the school parking lot. A crowd of parents, friends and relatives was waiting, and from that collection of welcomers a loud cheer went up. As soon as the bus stopped, happy campers jumped down and hugged their parents and guardians. Homecoming is a beautiful thing to witness.

Floyd and his co-chaperone had one last task to perform before heading home themselves. They made sure that nothing was left on board the bus, that all baggage had been claimed, and then they swept through the bus making sure that candy wrappers, soda bottles and detritus left behind was picked up. That completed, they thanked their driver for getting them back safely and went home. They had school early the next day.

The first "April in Paris" trip to Paris for Saratoga's students had been a success. During the thirty-seven years of his teaching career, Dr. Sarvey and his fellow chaperones took fifteen other trips, one almost every other year. It has been estimated that over seven hundred students took part in those trips, and Floyd's two children, Brooks and Janine, participated in at least two. Floyd's son, Brooks, served as a chaperone on two of those trips after serving four years as a United States Marine. Every one of the seven hundred or so participants returned safely to their home town. No accidents ever occurred which could have marred a perfect record. Ah, but there were moments worth mentioning...such as...

CHAPTER 15

Susan's Story

If you are ever in charge of a group of fifty teenagers whom you are escorting to another country, there are unmentionables one does not want to occur. A student struck by an automobile and seriously injured, a bus accident along a country road where more than one passenger suffers serious physical damage or worse, or one of the travelers, boy or girl, is physically attacked by a politically or religiously-motivated person. These are things not pointed out in a meeting of prospective travelers, but they are discussed privately by chaperones contemplating a trip abroad. But, if there is one phrase a teacher/chaperone does not want to hear, it is, "Someone is missing."

In the mid-80's, several trips had already taken place in the Saratoga Springs City Schools, and the success of the program required that only upperclassmen would be considered for the "April in Paris" excursions. Preparation meetings took place on a once-a-month basis, and these later trips through the

80's and 90's took participants to other parts of France instead of staying entirely in the French Capital. The student clientele for this particular trip included Floyd's two children, Brooks, now a senior, and Janine, a sophomore in high school. But, there was one student, a senior girl, who was suspect from the start.

Susan, a senior girl enrolled in one of Dr. Sarvey's French 5 classes, was different. Students in this advanced-French class were treated to a college-level course in the target language. Most all of the students enrolled in that class had developed the competency of a college sophomore in the subject...except Susan. Perhaps it was the girl's overly-shy nature. She lived with her mother, a single parent, who worked hard and earned her living as a salesperson in a department store. The mother seemed to be struggling economically, but she loved her daughter to the point that it was Sue to be the first to hand in her application and payment for the Paris trip. Floyd knew that Susan's timidity was holding her back in her effort to fully socialize with others, but her peers were above average in maturity and self-confidence; there was safety in numbers. No problem.

Once in country, students, chaperones and adult passengers did the usual. They visited monuments, churches, museums, and they shopped for souvenirs. The Eiffel Tower was climbed...(just a little after 7 P.M.), guards at the Tomb of the Unknown French Soldier were asked to supply the name of the person buried under the eternal flame, and portraits were commissioned at the artists' square in

Montmartre. A side trip was made to Chartres Cathedral, and everyone had an opportunity to compare that gothic church with Notre Dame in Paris. A two-day tour of the famous chateaux in the Loire Valley was also added before spending the last two days back in Paris before departure for the United States.

Back in Paris, near the last days in France, on a warm April evening, Floyd walked his entire group, students and adults, into the Latin Quarter. The balmy atmosphere and the Easter vacation had brought out hundreds of French university students and visitors from other countries into the now animated quarter. Late that evening, wall-to-wall humanity was enjoying the religious holiday season. Outdoor and open-air restaurants and bistros were bustling with patrons. Lines formed at every pasty shop. It was at that point that Floyd issued orders that everyone stick together and hold on to each other's elbow. They were even told to keep their eyes on the feet of the person in front of them. But, there were too many feet.

When it was time to head back to the hotel, this time located on the outskirts of the city, the Sarvey platoon climbed aboard their metro car and the train took off toward the hotel's stop. Group captains, selected to keep track of everyone in their pod of ten, began to count heads. One of the captains spoke up and said, "Dr. Sarvey, we're missing one person. It's Sue."

At the next metro stop, Floyd asked his colleague, Mr. Fontaine, to escort the rest of the troop to the hotel. He then commandeered two of his senior boys, both high-school athletes, got off the train and took the metro back in the opposite direction toward the Latin Quarter. Locating his lost sheep, Susan, the most vulnerable of his flock, was now a mission to be accomplished.

When Floyd and his two helpers arrived back at the quarter, the crowd of late-night revelers had swollen. Sticking together, the three searchers scanned the sea of humanity making its way around the square hoping to catch sight of a young American girl seeking help. In a final last-ditch effort, Floyd sought out and found a patrol of French policemen monitoring the evening's festivities. He approached the gendarmes and asked them if they had encountered any young American women needing assistance. A shrug of the shoulders followed by a polite response indicated that no such situation had come up during their watch. Floyd handed one of the officers a card with Sue's name, the name, number and address of his hotel in case the men encountered his lost student later in the evening. A replica of that card had been issued to everyone in the Saratoga group for just such emergencies. That card, later in the evening, proved to be one of the best and most fortuitous decisions made during the trip. It was at that moment, however, that dark and ominous thoughts were brought to mind.

In his enlistment as a young Marine, Floyd had been stationed at the Brooklyn Navy Yard as a sentinel. While there, the base had been used as a coming home port for Marines stationed in Europe. He remembered talking to some of these fellow jarheads who had just returned from Embassy duty in Port Lyautey, French Morocco. Like many others in that Moroccan city, young men, in their off-duty hours, frequented the bars and *les bordels*, establishments of ill repute. In one of those places, the Marines had encountered a couple of American girls who, while traveling alone in Europe, had been taken by force, placed aboard a ship in Marseilles, and shipped to North Africa to serve as prostitutes until too old to do so. The Marines were told by the girls that trying to free them from this forced slavery was useless, and that, if they tried, they would be killed. Floyd immediately saw himself staying behind in France and making his way across the Mediterranean to French Morocco to find his lost female. He also knew that returning to Saratoga without one of his students was out of the question.

The Paris metro shuts down its trains and services at midnight. In one final last effort, Floyd stopped at a Latin Quarter bistro and asked the manager if he could use the establishment's phone. In the mid-80's, Americans had not yet become prisoners of their cell phones, and the manager of the bistro was pleased to be helpful. Floyd made a call to his hotel. To his surprise, instead of the hotel's desk clerk, it was Mr. Fontaine who answered. Fontaine said, "She's here. Come back to the hotel." No questions were asked. Floyd and his two companions caught the last train and made their way back to the hotel.

Waiting in the hotel lobby was Mr. Fontaine and a woman whom Floyd did not recognize. The woman introduced herself saying that she, like Floyd and his colleague, was a teacher of French from some mid-western town conducting her student group through Paris. She had been in the Latin Quarter that evening when a distraught, tearful young American girl had run headlong into her arms asking for help. Sue had showed her hotel card and identification explaining that she had gotten separated from her peers and needed help. The woman, now an American savior, hired a taxi and escorted Sue back to the Saratoga hotel where the rest of the group was waiting at the hotel lobby.

A very sincere thanks was offered the woman who had so kindly lent a helping hand. In a conversation with Floyd, the teacher/tour guide told him that Sue had been approached by two unsavory men who had offered to take her to their apartment for safekeeping. That's when she bolted and ran directly into the American woman's arms. Floyd thanked his fellow professional, and paid her way by taxi to her own hotel in the city. Thanks to a hotel card carried by everyone in the Saratoga group and a friendly American fellow teacher, a long stay in France and a sea crossing into North Africa was avoided.

For the rest of the stay in Paris, Floyd's daughter, Janine, then just a high school sophomore, was assigned as a personal shadow for Sue. Janine never left her side the rest of the trip, and everyone in that year's "April in Paris" trip returned safely home, and that made possible continued trips to *La Belle France.*

As a footnote, four years later, Sue, the lost soul, encountered Floyd in downtown Saratoga. She walked up to her former teacher and announced, "Dr. Sarvey, I just spent the summer in France...alone." It was nice being there for that one, and Sue's story is testament of good human growth and development.

Brook's portrait at Place Du Tertre

CHAPTER 16

Dutch Pastries and Other Delicacies

In an effort to make the price of travel affordable to as many students as possible, Floyd and his fellow teacher investigated different airline companies and travel agencies. One year, KLM advertised flights going to Amsterdam, Holland and continuing to Paris via bus. Flying into another European country and then on to France appealed to many, and before too long, another Saratoga "April in Paris" excursion was up and running.

The landing in Amsterdam was colorful. The Dutch use every bit of land given them, and the fields running up to the very runways of the airport were as if someone had blanketed them with multicolored flowers. Windmills rose up out of the ground and offered another unusual but interesting aspect of this country salvaged from the sea. Once through customs, everyone boarded a bus and headed for Paris.

On the bus, familiar chatter took place, and it was announced that on the return trip, again out of Amsterdam, a full day and night would be spent in that city. For the moment, however, all looked forward to being the first to spot the Eiffel Tower. It was still four hundred miles before anyone would catch sight of the monument, and it was time to check passports. The busload of passengers were asked to hold up their official travel documents, and all but one student did as they were told.

Sitting in the rear of the bus, one senior boy started patting the pockets of his sport jacket as if he was putting out a small fire. Yep, sure enough, the boy had dropped his passport somewhere back in the airport or worse, it was on a plane flying to some other country. Floyd explained to the young man and to the other passengers that as soon as the group arrived in Paris, the boy would make the acquaintance of some Marine embassy guards in charge of helping people get a new passport. The boy did just that the next day. That same young man became the Saratoga County District Attorney and then the County Court Judge. Whether he still has an up-to-date passport is not known.

In the City of Light, the usual Parisian highlights were enjoyed. The chateaux in the Loire Valley, Chartres Cathedral and a quick stop at Mont St. Michel, the Christian church/fortress from which William the Conqueror left in 1066 on his way to Hastings in England was enjoyed. The *piece de resistance* in that monument's restaurants is a French omelet cooked to perfection. More than one person in the Saratoga group learned to love the dish of beaten eggs cooked and folded. Then, it was back to Paris with special instructions that students would spend their free days in groups of three to four people. Floyd did not want to think about crossing the Mediterranean in search of a missing student.

On this one trip, one of Floyd's former students, now a college graduate and local business man, was one of the group's adult travelers. This young man, Al, had been in the very first class that Floyd had taught in Saratoga, and he could recite verbatim the speech given that first day in class by his former teacher. Al made at least one other trip with his former teacher, but this time, a special happening took place.

The students and adult travelers were told that the Parisian pickpockets were the best in the world, and that they should carry currency, passports and other valuables in a money belt. Many followed that advice. Al did not. One evening when he and Floyd were on a crowded metro car on their way to Montmartre, Al stated that he was wearing tight blue jeans, so tight that his travel checks were mashed tightly to the inside of his front pocket. Just about that time, the car pulled into its stop, and a group of young unshaven men got on and bushed up against both Floyd and Al. Nothing was said, apologies were made and the car went on to the next stop. As soon as the car pulled into the next station, the three men got off, and the train started up again. A Frenchman standing alongside Al got his attention pointing to the floor by Al's feet. There, in a neat little bundle were Al's travelers' checks. The kind Frenchman explained that the three men who had left the train performed their magic, and when they noticed that the checks had not been signed, they threw them on the floor and left the train. Floyd jokingly suggested that Al put his checks in his socks for safekeeping.

Al was not the only notable Saratoga townsperson to travel with that year's tour. The president of one of Saratoga's prominent banks was with Floyd and Al at the artists' quarter in Montmartre on one sunny day watching students and others get their portraits done. Floyd had recounted the story of Al's tight blue jeans and his travelers' checks. The three men were sitting at an outdoor table having a cool beverage when the bank president spoke up saying, "I have a foolproof method of preventing any pickpocket from hitting me up. I keep my paper currency pinned to the inside of my jacket pocket. I use a big safety pin." Just to show his mastery over the finite skill of Parisian pickpockets, he patted his jacket pocket. The look of surprise which appeared on the bank president's face said it all. Inspecting the inside of his pocket, he did find the safety pin. The money was gone. Floyd just had to say, "Man, that works well doesn't it."

The next day, Floyd's tour group left the French Capital and headed for Amsterdam looking forward to the flight home from that city. But, before departure, a day and night's stay in the constitutional capital of the Netherlands would take place. When the bus pulled into the hotel where the group would spend the night, they discovered that the building was at least a couple hundred years old, and without an elevator. Some of the older members of the Saratoga group were placed in rooms on the third floor of the building and a rickety narrow wooden staircase was the only way to get to some of the rooms. Once again, Al and some of the senior high students saved the day by acting as pack mules. But, there was a silver lining; the group had been promised that the evening's meal would take place in a favorite eating place serving a special Indonesian cuisine. The special place was the Kaloon Restaurant. So, around dinner time, off they went.

The large Saratoga family was ushered into the Kaloon and seated theater style with dining tables facing the food preparation area. In front of this kitchen setup, two long tables had been made ready to hold food which would be distributed to the guests by servers. On both tables, two large ceramic serving pots filled with a steaming hot vegetable-soup like mixture were placed in full view, and in each pot, there was a long-handled ladle. Floyd and Al had front seats facing the food tables, and they waited as servers milled about carrying large platters of cooked and seasoned rice. That's when the monster from the Black Lagoon made its appearance.

From out of the depths of one of the soup bowls in front of them emerged the head of something the size of a thumb. But, this thumb had eyes and feelers. The thing made its way to the handle of the ladle, and started its climb out of the hot liquid and on to the end of the handle. From there, it dropped to the table's surface, made its way to the end of the table and dropped onto the floor. Perhaps energized by the still steaming liquid in the bowl, it continued its march toward the other side of the room. Al looked at his former teacher and said, "Was that part of the entertainment?" None of the other diners seemed to have witnessed the miraculous escape the bug had made, but, Floyd and Al did not touch the soup that evening.

After dinner, the troop went back to the hotel and prepared for the next morning's departure. But, the night wasn't over. On one of the landings on the second floor, there seemed to be some commotion near one of the large windows looking out on to the buildings next door. Directly across the street, now at eye level and sitting in the windowsills, several scantily-clad young women, bathed in red lights were gyrating to the sound of music and beckoning to passers-by as they did so. One of Sarvey's students said, "Dr. Sarvey, what are those women doing?" Some snickers erupted from some of the older boys and girls now eyeballing the show next door. Sarvey, not to be outdone, replied, "It must be some department store clothing promotion. Better make sure everything is packed for tomorrow's departure." The next morning, everyone had a story to tell on the way back to the United States, and everyone returned safely to Saratoga.

CHAPTER 17

Second Sight and the Ghost

The year 1984, besides being the title of George Orwell's book predicting social change, was important to Floyd Sarvey. His program of foreign language studies at his Upstate New York public secondary school had drawn the attention of other professionals in his field. His program in French at the public-school level brought special recognition to both him and his school. In the fall of the year, The New York State Association of Teachers of Foreign Language had named Sarvey as the recipient of the "Ruth E. Wasley Distinguished Teacher of the Year Award in the State of New York". But, there was still more to be accomplished, and another "April in Paris" tour was being planned. This year was a special one.

Floyd's daughter, Janine, was in her senior year of high school, and her father had enjoyed the special opportunity of teaching Janine and her brother, Brooks, on two separate occasions while they took classes at Saratoga High. Floyd often told his wife, Marilyn, that he was able to spend as much time with their children as did the mother.

During her high school career, Janine had developed into an athlete. She played softball, basketball and volleyball. A lot of her friends who also studied French were among those who had signed up for this year's trip to France, and that added to the excitement which took place in planning meetings. That excitement was soon going to manifest itself in an otherworldly way.

Familiar steps leading up to the 1985 tour began to take shape. Things learned from past excursions were applied and given out as information in the monthly meetings attended by all the travelers. Floyd continued to stick by his word that the school's administration and its board of education would not play a role in the planning. The father of one of Floyd's students was a board of education member, and French trips had gained so much recognition, that the father suggested that he petition the board for approval and authorization for upcoming flights abroad. Floyd realized, however, that the board's recognition and approval might also entail rule changes and result in lesser adherence to discipline. Floyd liked the old adage, "If it isn't broken, don't fix it." He stuck to holding his planning meetings at the public library.

As soon as Janine's group arrived in Paris, Floyd's daughter acted as tour guide for her friends. It was Janine's third trip to France, and she was already knowledgeable about what to ask and not to ask of the guards at the Tomb of the Unknown Soldier, and she knew how to look for and pick out the perfect artist in the Place

Du Tertre in Montmartre. This year, she had a special souvenir in mind---a portrait drawn by one of the artists at Montmartre.

One bright sunny morning on a students' free day, Janine escorted her friends to the artists' square. She taught her peers how to seek out and barter with an artist whose work looked more skilled than others. That accomplished, she picked out a man whom she thought had captured a certain *Je ne sais quoi* in his subjects. Little did she know that the artist was a little like George Orwell; he could see the future.

In 1890, Oscar Wilde, the English writer and bon vivant, whose tomb was visited by past and present Saratoga students in the Pere Lachaise Cemetery in Paris, wrote a short story entitled, "The Picture of Dorian Gray". In that story, Dorian Gray, a corrupt young man, commissioned a portrait. In the beginning, the picture was acceptable. As time went on, the image depicted in the painting changed year by year and began to reflect the evilness of the subject and his corruptible life. Just the opposite took place in the portrait Janine had requested in Montmartre.

In her high school years, Janine had developed the body and looks of an athlete. Sturdy, heavily built and ready for action, Janine even played rugby in her freshman year in college. But, the Parisian artist captured a different physiognomy in the subject who sat for her portrait. The compieted drawing showed a mature, svelte young woman fully confident in her ability to take on the challenge of womanhood. When Floyd first saw the finished portrait that day in Montmartre, he questioned the artist's talent.

Now, years later, he realizes that Janine's artist was Orwellian in his ability capture beauty, and the end result was a complete antithesis of the story of Dorian Gray. But, the magic was yet to come.

Near the middle of that 1985 trip, the Saratoga group went into the Loire Valley to take in the magnificent chateaux built during the sixteenth and seventeenth centuries. French kings and their entourage needed a cooling off place where they could escape the summer heat in Paris. At one such chateau, Chambord, the group toured a four-hundred room palace. To get to the upper floors, a double spiraled staircase allowed Janine and her friends to see each other going up and coming down yet not touching or being close to one another. As they passed each other on the staircase, they *"Rebonjoured"* their friends on the other side of the stone steps. But, the real attraction or specter was yet to come.

The next stop on the tour took place at the Chateau de Chenonceau, the large palace built by Henri II in 1514. A direct descendent of Richard the Lionhearted, Henri II was married to Catherine de Medici. But, Henri had a mistress, Diane de Poitiers, and it was for her that the chateau was built. When Henri II died, the result of a jousting accident, Catherine de Medici moved her husband's mistress out and took over the chateau. All portraits of the mistress were destroyed and in their place, the likeness of Catherine reigned supreme. During WW I, the chateau served as a hospital for French wounded soldiers, and since the chateau spanned the River Cher, its interior allowed the crossing of the river by French underground forces in WW

II. Now, however, it offered up another aspect of the past.

The bus carrying Saratoga's students, chaperones and other adult tour goers pulled into the chateau in the early afternoon. Guides gave the group an oral overview of the chateau's history and its long-dead inhabitants. Then, everyone was left on their own to explore the rooms and the period furniture of the dwelling. Janine seemed ready to do the exploring on her own. About thirty minutes into the free time, Janine called out to her father and said, "Dad, I have to go outside, and I have to go now." Floyd asked whether she was ill. Janine said, "I'll talk to you about it later." She left the chateau and waited outside the entrance and collected what remained of her self-confidence.

In conversations later that afternoon and in later years, Janine explained what had occurred. She had been wandering alone through the long hallway on the first floor of the chateau when she came on to an open stairway leading to the second-floor bedrooms. She started up the stairs when she saw something or someone standing at the top of the stairway looking down at her and smiling. The figure was that of a woman in the clothing of the fifteen hundreds, clothing she had seen in paintings at the Louvre. She said the figure seemed to be bathed in a mist-like shimmering light, and then it disappeared completely as if the power of an electric light had been turned off.

Before the group left, Floyd accompanied Janine back into the chateau and climbed the stairs into a bedroom area. At the back of the room, a portrait of Catherine de Medici hung on the wall. Janine said, "Dad, that's the lady I saw at the top of the stairs." Had she seen a *revenant?* Could it have been the ghost of a woman who wanted everyone to know that the Chateau de Chenonceau was still hers? We are not sure. But there is one thing for certain. If Janine ever accompanies her own daughter, Marley, to the Valley of the Loire, there is one chateau which will be on the list of things to see, talk about, and experience. There might even be a familiar face or two.

Chenonceau – Janine's ghost chateau

CHAPTER 18

The Ambulant Blue Comb

In the course of a man's life, the male of the species usually makes only a few very close friends. In the games played, in preparing himself as a warrior either in actual combat, on the field of play or in taking part in friendly get togethers, a man sometimes has difficulty adjusting to those like him. There seems to be a competitive spirit which sometimes inspires an unwillingness in some men to share the limelight with others of his own kind. This is a story about the opposite side of such feelings.

Floyd Sarvey arrived for the first time in Saratoga Springs and attended his first teacher-orientation meeting at the beginning of the school year. Only one of the several members of his department came forward and introduced himself. That one person was Rolland Fontaine, a fellow teacher of French. Some others in Floyd's department were not quite sure that they wanted a newcomer, an out-of-stater, to represent them as head of the department. Sarvey wasn't even a native Saratogian. He was an upstart from a big university in Pennsylvania. That did not stop Rolland Fontaine from stepping up to Floyd and saying, "My name is Rolland Fontaine. I am one of your colleagues. Welcome to Saratoga."

Floyd's recollection of Rolland was simple---the man always had a smile on his face. In his days and years working with Rolland, Floyd had never heard him use a harsh word about anyone. If a conversation took place where criticism of another was being expressed, Rolland would immediately change the subject or move away from those in protest. The man loved his job. He loved teaching his target language and he loved his wife, Theresa. Life was his drug of preference. Knowing this, Floyd often asked himself why he decided to play a practical joke on such a man.

About thirty years ago, early in his career as department head of foreign languages, Floyd was wrapping up his day at the end of school. Rolland was still in his classroom, and Floyd had to do some work in the school library. On his way back from the library, the school hallways were loaded with debris. Things dropped during the course of the day were everywhere. Bits of paper, lost homework assignments, half-filled lunch bags, pencils, pens and other things dropped by students hurrying to and fro while changing classes now littered the hallways. And, among this flotsam thrown up by waves of students during the day was a large, blue plastic comb.

Floyd's first reaction was to avoid even giving the thing a second glance. Who knew where such a thing had been? Ah, but all of a sudden, nothing like that mattered. That comb was meant for better things, and Floyd knew exactly where it was going to go. Using a piece of scrap paper, he retrieved the comb from the detritus on the floor and carried it to the faculty men's washroom where the comb was cleansed of anything harmful. He returned to the department office and studied the surroundings.

Rolland Fontaine was still working in his classroom. But, his winter coat, hat and gloves were hanging near his desk. On the floor, Rolland's heavy overshoe-type boots with metal buckles running up the front drew his attention. Floyd picked up one of the boots and knew exactly what to do. Using some masking tape, a commodity readily available to most classroom teachers, Floyd fastened the blue comb securely to the sole of one of the boots. He returned the boot alongside its mate, and sat back and prepared the next day's lesson.

Before long, Fontaine came into the department office and began his preparation to leave for the day. Some things were said about the day's happenings as Floyd's teaching partner was putting his winter coat, hat and gloves in place. Next came the boots. The hitchhiker comb held securely in place, and Rolland started his trek out into the hallway toward the school's exit. As he made his way down the tiled hallway, Floyd detected a "click, click, click" of the comb's contact with the hard surface of the hallway. The sound of plastic contacting with the solid hallway floor continued, and Floyd continued his work at his desk. But, things do have a way of boomeranging.

Several days passed without a word ever being said by either man about what had transpired at the end of the school day some time before. Any guilt Floyd might have felt about the little joke he had played dissipated, and day to day lesson planning and teaching washed the mind's memory of any wrongdoing. However, two weeks later, winter's cold snap had not finished, and winter clothing was again going to play a role in a reappearance of the blue traveler.

It was Floyd's turn to leave early at the end of the school day. His fleece-lined raincoat firmly buttoned up to his neck, briefcase in hand, Floyd made his way out to the school parking lot. He opened his car door and sat down in the driver's seat when he uttered, "Holy ----!" Something had jabbed at him through his trousers from under his seat. He checked. Nothing! Whatever it was must have fallen to the floor, but he could see nothing out of place when he got out of the car to check. He re-entered his automobile, and there it was again---the same jagging sensation he had felt previously. He once again exited his car and checked his coat pockets. Nothing. He checked the lining of the coat. There was something stuck in the lining of the coat. Fingering a small hole in the lining, he discovered a long, thin piece of plastic. The comb had resurfaced.

The next day, it was impossible to withhold the news of the comb's return. The story of its meandering ways was related to others in the department office as everyone gathered for the beginning of the school day. Some of Floyd's colleagues laughed, some questioned the antics of the two seemingly mature staff members and then, everyone went about their business of teaching their target languages. A prank had been played on the nicest man on the faculty, Mr. Fontaine, but, all's well that ends well. But, certain things have a way of continuing, and the blue comb was itching to act up again.

A month or two later, the school custodians were in the process of replacing classroom ceiling lights. To accomplish their task, tall ladders were brought into Mr. Fontaine's classroom and stored in the back of the room for use the next day. The next morning, Floyd, always the first to arrive at school, spied the ladders. An *idee fixe* came to mind immediately. Moving one of the ladders to the middle of Fontaine's classroom, Floyd mounted it and using the ever-present masking tape, affixed the blue comb to the middle of the ceiling ten feet off the floor. Replacing the ladder to the rear of the classroom, Floyd returned to the department office and prepared for the day.

No mention of the high-flying ambulant comb was made for weeks. But, one day at the end of school, teachers had collected in the department office and were preparing to go home when Mr. Fontaine came in. He was laughing out loud, and when he was able, he announced to everyone there that one of his students had come up to his desk at the end of class and said, "Mr. Fontaine, do you know that there is a blue comb on the middle of your ceiling?" Everyone burst out in laughter. They knew what had happened, and they knew who had placed the blue monster in its lofty place.

A full year passed before the comb resurfaced. It had taken some time for Mr. Fontaine to petition the custodians to lend him one of their ladders. But, now, in an off year of travel, the Fontaines and the Sarveys decided to vacation at one of the Club Med villages in Martinique during the April vacation. Once there, sun, sand and sea were enjoyed by the husbands and wives. But, one day, Floyd, an avid snorkeler, wanted to explore the clear blue waters of the Caribbean. He sat down on the beach and began putting on his swim fins. But, there was a problem. He couldn't get his foot into one of them. Something was stuck in the fin's opening and prevented him from getting ready for the swim. Looking closely into the fin's opening, he discovered the problem. Lodged into the toe area of one fin was a dark, long, blue objet. The traveler had not remained back in New York.

Over the years, that now sacred blue piece of plastic has made its way to Canada, France, back to the Caribbean and beyond. It has been served under glass as an entrée in four-star restaurants, it has ridden on the Paris metro, visited the Louvre and been present at a mass in Notre Dame Cathedral. It has even been at the Chateau de Chenonceau and perhaps witnessed the ghost of Marie de Medici. And, it has served its purpose; it cemented a life-long friendship between two grown men. Where it now rests will be divulged in later chapters in this book.

CHAPTER 19

Kodak Flash Cubes and the Mommies

In most of the Saratoga "April in Paris" tours, Floyd had noticed that during the early first days in France, the entire caravan of travelers was physically exhausted from the thirty-hour effort to get to Europe. Excitement, expectation and the unknown played a role in sapping strength which resulted from lack of sleep. Arriving in France at eight o'clock in the morning did not help the situation; hotels could not admit guests until rooms had been cleaned, and that demanded that a bus tour of the city took place immediately upon landing.

On the bus, an elderly French woman acted as host/guide, and she did her best to point out the historic sites passing by out the windows of the bus. This woman, one of the kindest guides Floyd had encountered, paid special attention to Floyd's son, Brooks, now ten years old and making his first trip to France. The guide asked Brooks what he wanted to see when he visited the Louvre. "Mommies!", he said. And sure enough, the lady took him alone to that part of the museum which held the Egyptian exhibit. Floyd never forgot that kindness. Perhaps that's why he was so upset that the rest of his travelers were dead to the world on the bus going into the city.

If pedestrians on the streets had looked at the bus rolling by, they would have wondered why a busload of people who looked like they were being transferred to the morgue would be passing by in broad daylight. Open-mouthed, tongues hanging out, eyes rolled back into the head, drool dripping down chins---this was the scene that Floyd had offered to his history-giving guide. There was very little Sarvey could do. His troop was now in another world, and understood nothing that the guide was verbally offering. While Floyd understood the reason why his group was tired, he also knew that something had to be done in the days to come to encourage everyone to absorb what they had come to enjoy and learn.

The next day, taking another bus tour around the city, Floyd decided to use Brooks, his ten-year old, in an effort to maintain the attention of everyone on board. He asked Brooks to keep an eye open for those who began to slumber during the tour. It was his job to jostle the incapacitated and keep them awake. This, to a young boy, was like giving treats to a famished K-9. Like some Jack Russel terrier, Brooks went up and down the aisles bugging the older students who wanted to strangle the little guy. But, after a while, someone would nudge their friend and say, "Wake up! Brooks is coming."

In later years, after four years of serving as a United States Marine and graduating from the university, Brooks played another role for his father. While in the military, he had been on manoeuvers with his expeditionary unit in France, and his use of the target language served him well. When Floyd asked his son to accompany him on an "April in Paris" tour as a chaperone, he jumped at the chance. At one of the monthly meetings he introduced himself by saying, "The last time I was in France, I was in battle gear and carrying an automatic weapon." That seemed to get the attention of everyone very quickly, and when Brooks was on the trip, discipline was never a problem and everyone felt a little bit safer. But the problem of keeping everyone on task during bus rides still lingered. Ah, one picture is worth a thousand words.

Floyd had recently invested in a Canon Sure Shot camera, and it required four-sided flash cubes. One day aboard the bus, he announced that, in the future, documentation of all sleeping beauties would take place, and that pictures captured of all the horrible configurations of one's face would be available for all to see back in his classroom once everyone returned from the trip. He enhanced the threat of such things by saying, "If you feel the heat of a flash cube on your face while caught open-mouthed, tongue out and the sun highlighting the drool running down your chin, it's too late; your picture has been taken." That announcement kept everyone's attention on the guide's explanation of historic places for a short while. However, when up late discussing things with other students instead of getting a good night's rest, one forgets such warnings.

In the days to come, photographic masterpieces were collected. Some of them so horrible that students would roll with laughter when Floyd's camera shed light on the Quasimodo-like faces captured on film. But, there is a winner in every contest, and it was one of Floyd's colleagues, Sheila, an elementary school teacher, who garnered first prize. On one bright, sunny afternoon on the way to Chartres Cathedral by bus, a student tapped Floyd on the shoulder and said, "Dr. Sarvey, you should see this." The student pointed to Sheila, now almost prone in her seat, head thrown back in abandon, mouth open showing a huge wad of gum, tongue hanging out like some trout in a fisherman's basket, and a long string of drool dripping like some rain spout into a cistern. It was a classic opportunity. When Floyd's flash went off, Sheila's eyes opened as if she had been hit with a cattle prod. She exclaimed, "Floyd, you didn't!" He responded, "I had to. That photo could qualify to hang in the Louvre."

In the days to come, Sheila asked others around her what she must have looked like. Her friends enhanced their description of what the facial scene was like by saying, "Your picture is going to take first prize. No other will come close." That, of course, did not help things. Sheila told Floyd that she would pay any price for the photo and its negative. He answered that all the pictures were going to be judged by students in the school's cafeteria once they returned but that no one's picture could compete with hers. As soon as the group arrived home,

Floyd sent both the original and its negative to Sheila's home. She thanked him by phone two days later saying, "That photo and its partner are now located in the town's landfill."

Students on future trips did not have to be told about the roving camera. They had heard the story. And, now, so have you.

CHAPTER 20

End-of-Career Reminiscences

In thinking back over his years in the classroom and second-language teaching, Floyd thought he would be negligent if some of the more positive aspects of his time with others was left out. He had found that parents, in almost every case, will go to great lengths to give their children opportunities they themselves did not have. Some of the adults with whom Floyd had come in contact were not well off financially. Yet, these fathers and mothers sacrificed to send their sons and daughters on ten-day trips to France. Some of these caring parents would not take the time and/or money to treat themselves to an outing at the beach, but they would save for a year or more to make sure their children had a chance to climb the Eiffel Tower with their friends.

In one case, a well-known local contractor took his wife and two sons on one of the "April in Paris" tours. He could just as easily have taken the trip alone with his family, but he wanted to see his sons enjoy the company of their peers on such an outing. One day during the tour in Paris, the father overheard Floyd talking to his colleague, Mr. Fontaine, about whether a dinner cruise on the Seine in the *bateaux mouches* might be possible. These tourist boats made such trips at night, and sumptuous meals were served during the tour. But, money for such a thing was not in Floyd's budget. The next day, the hometown-builder handed Floyd forty-eight tickets for the evening dinner tour on the boats. Everyone had dinner that evening as they motored up the Seine and passed a well-lighted Eiffel Tower and Notre Dame Cathedral. The man asked nothing in return for his magnanimity other than the pleasure of seeing his wife and sons enjoy the company of other Saratogians sail up the Seine River and have dinner together on an excursion boat.

There were other surprises, too. In spite of the fact that strict rules applied to the consumption of alcohol while on his trips and in adherence to parental-permission slips granting their sons and daughters one glass of wine at dinner, things do happen. One day while walking through the *grandes salles* of the Louvre with his students, Floyd heard a bottle hit the floor. One of his senior girls sheepishly bent over and picked up her empty souvenir bottle of Stella Artois, one of the premium beers in Europe. Floyd said to his student, "That must have come from ceiling. Watch your head." The student was allowed to keep her souvenir.

Floyd also learned of his students' versatility. One day, his busload of students and adults was making its way through one of the older villages near the Loire Valley. The village streets were very narrow and parked on both sides were small French-made automobiles. The bus driver was worried that his vehicle could not make it through the maze of small cars and continue on its tour. No problem. A group of senior boys stepped up and said, "Dr. Sarvey, we can take care of that for you." Four or five boys got off the bus, picked up one small car after the other and moved them onto the sidewalk. The French bus driver exclaimed, "*Ah, ces Americains! Incroyable!*" Floyd thought the same thing; Americans are incredible.

Lessons in language learning often took place. Students learned that what they had studied in the classroom actually worked in the streets of France. They could make people understand their use of the language, and this skill worked especially well in the patisseries, restaurants and at the Tomb of the Unknown French Soldier under the Arch of Triumph. And, the discovery of such skills was at times amusing. Floyd's daughter, Janine, was eight years old when she made her first trip with her father's group. One day, outside her hotel, she caught sight of some young French children playing in the street, and wanted to join them. After a while, she returned to her mother's side and said, "Wow, Mom, those children must really be smart. They already know how to speak French. How did they learn it so fast?" That discovery brought smiles to the faces of those listening. There were other amusing anecdotes as well.

One of Floyd's former students, Eric, taught art at the same high school. Eric and his wife,

Sue, had become popular with many students by organizing "Art Nights" much like "Foreign Language Nights" which took place in the past. Floyd asked Eric if he and his wife might act as chaperones on an upcoming trip. They both agreed, and Eric was put in charge with a sum of money which was going to be used for tips for the French guides and for emergencies when needed. Eric asked his former teacher how he was to carry this reserve of currency. Floyd said, "Well, Eric, in the Corps, we couldn't use our pockets for anything but ammunition, so we used our socks to carry needed currency. For the entire ten-day's stay in France, when money was needed, Floyd would say, "Eric, get your foot ready!" That bulge around Eric's ankle came in handy of many occasions.

At the time of this written record of one man's influence on the teaching of second languages at the secondary and university level, we are at the end of the second decade of the twenty-first century. Dr. Sarvey ended his high-school career in 2001, and his university-level career five years later. Now, he plays pickle ball with his wife and against much younger players. He seems to be able to hold his own with anyone ten or twenty years younger. He no longer jumps from planes with a parachute. He is able to play "Foggy Mountain Breakdown" and other songs on his banjo, and he can hit some blues notes on his harmonica. Watching Penn State football games with his favorite cheerleader, Marilyn, takes up some fall Saturday afternoons, and happy hours, only on days which end in "day" are enjoyed. Every so often, an opinion of political misdoings and social changes takes place in letters with his name affixed and sent to the editor of some newspapers, and he keeps in touch with those with whom he worked.

Shortly after his retirement, Floyd's daughter, Janine, put together a generous sum of money and established with the Administration of the Saratoga Springs City Schools, an endowment fund for the "Floyd A. Sarvey Excellence in Foreign Language Award" which goes to a senior boy or girl who excelled in a second language over a four-year period. The recipient receives a check for $250.00 which is used for whatever the winner, chosen by members of the foreign language department, wishes. A large plaque commemorating Sarvey, complete with his picture and spaces for twenty names or more of award winners, hangs in a prominent place in the school's hallway. One evening, after a night of lip-sync singing of French songs, Floyd and his wife stopped by the plaque to review the names of past winners of the award. Others, a mother and her daughter, were admiring the picture as well. Sarvey spoke to the woman and asked, "Do you know anything about the person pictured on the plaque?" The woman replied, "Oh, he's dead." Sarvey said, "Really, he looks so young." The woman then compared the picture with the man beside her and uttered, "Oh, I'm so sorry!" Floyd answered, "That's OK. I'm not."

In the summer of 2018, Rolland E. Fontaine, Floyd's colleague for more than twenty-five years, died. Rolland was eighty-seven years old, and enjoyed life with his wife, Theresa. Floyd and his wife, Marilyn, made sure that the largest display of flowers at Rolland's wake came from them. At that viewing of the body, Floyd brought with him a large, blue plastic comb, something picked up in the detritus of a school hallway. Floyd used that trinket to play jokes on his friend at school. It had traveled to France, Canada, Martinique, Guadeloupe and other places. It had been given back and forth to one another and ended up in dining places, pieces of clothing, swim fins, and mailboxes. Rolland's wife, Theresa, was well aware of the comb's history and importance between her husband and Floyd. At the viewing of Rolland's body and standing next to Theresa and her husband's open casket, he pulled out the comb from his suit jacket and said to his former colleague's wife, "What do I do with this?" Knowing what Floyd was asking, she quickly said, "Put it in there." That comb, and its memory will rest in his friend's coffin in perpetuity, but the memory of being there will last for as long as those who continue to read books.

CHAPTER 21

Kennedy Half Dollars and Wolfgang Puck

On at least one planning session or monthly meeting leading up to "April in Paris" tours for his students, Floyd would always include the topic of French cuisine. Most Americans are aware of the mystic associated with French cooking, and thousands of American households contain a copy of Julia Child's, *The Joy of French Cooking.* Knowing that, Floyd made reference to *soupe a l'oignon*, the croque monsieur, and the *sandwicheries* found in every quarter in Paris. In his classes at school, students were taught how to make and enjoy some of these classic less-expensive foods. Once in France, his students would have no trouble ordering familiar French-edibles.

Some of the more famous eating establishments were mentioned, but going to such places was not usually affordable on a student's budget. For some of the adults on the trip, however, nothing was impossible. Everyone was told about the "Tour d'Argent", the famous third-floor restaurant overlooking the Seine River and Notre Dame Cathedral. "Chez Marius", the exclusive restaurant frequented by French politicians located directly behind the National Assembly in Paris was also brought up. And, yes, the "Jules Verne", a restaurant *de luxe* located on the second floor of the Eiffel Tower was outlined. But, in the early 70's, there was one special place, a restaurant which was much too expensive for a secondary-school teacher to even consider, and that was Maxim's.

Maxim's is located at No. 3 rue Royale just off Place de la Concorde and close to the American Embassy. The restaurant is known for its Art Nouveau décor characterized by sinuous lines, foliate forms, stained-glass windows and a well-dressed clientele. At one time, Maxim's was regarded as the most famous restaurant in the world. Founded in 1893 by Maxime Gaillard, a former waiter, it began to thrive as a favorite eating place. It became so famous that the third act of Franz Lehar's 1905 operetta, "The Merry Widow" was set there. During the German occupation of France, 1941-1944, Maxim's was the official restaurant of the German high command. Nothing was ever rationed at that restaurant during the war years. But, this was 1973, and Floyd's first "April in Paris" group was in France.

Floyd, his fellow adult travelers and his students did not know it at the time, but Maxim's had attracted a lot of VIP's and jet-setters. In 1970, Brigitte Bardot caused a scandal when she entered the restaurant barefoot. A year of two later, Sylvie Vartan, the French pop singer; John Travolta; Jeanne Moreau, the French actress/singer; and Barbara Streisand graced the premises. Who would have guessed that an American teacher's wife would have had lunch there?

In a previous chapter of this book, an adult woman traveler on Floyd's tour thought that the word, "PRIVE!", was a place where one could relieve oneself of body wastes. Yes, that woman! She was still on this trip. Let's call her, Mary. Perhaps it had to do with Floyd's special attention to Mary's concerns or perhaps she enjoyed the disposition and kindness of Floyd's wife, but Mary reached out to Marilyn in a wonderful way.

Mary was a well-off Saratogian whose family business was thriving. The adults had a free day coming up, and Mary suggested to Marilyn that she be her guest at Maxim's for lunch. Floyd had no such free day. His hours were spent showing his students how to barter with artists in the Place du Tertre and have their portraits drawn. Making sure that lost passports were replaced at the American Embassy also took some time. Little things, but necessary ones had to be taken care of, and there was no way lunch could be ordered at Maxim's. For "Mary of the Privy", money was no object, and he appreciated the woman's offer of taking Marilyn to the restaurant. And, in that special place, a certain kind of money was to play another role.

When John F. Kennedy visited France in the early 60's, the French were in love with the American President. He had fought in the Pacific during WWII, he was an intellectual, and he was a bright, new political force. But, his strongest point, at least for the French, was his wife, Jacqueline; she spoke perfect French. At Versailles Palace, during the official welcoming ceremony, Mrs. Kennedy expressed her thanks for the kindness of the French, and she did so in their language. When the President was assassinated in 1963, the American government authorized that a coin be struck commemorating the President. The Kennedy Half Dollar arrived, and "Mary of the Privy" had a sac full of them with her in Paris.

When the day came for the two American woman to go to lunch at Maxim's, Floyd confirmed reservations by phone. Both women dressed in their finest, and they set off to experience lunch at one of the best-known restaurants in the world. Floyd reminded the ladies to be back at their hotel by 6 P.M. where a bus would be waiting to take the group to a different restaurant for dinner. That completed, the two women walked a short distance of a couple city blocks to Maxim's.

The girls arrived at the restaurant just before their reservation time of one o'clock. A doorman greeted them with a bow, opened the door and ushered them in. Both women were immediately struck with an unaccustomed opulence of the restaurant's décor. Saratoga had some fine restaurants, but nothing matched the lavishness of Maxim's. Swept up by the major-domo and two waiters, the women were escorted to their table, seated and served an aperitif. Mary, in appreciation for the prompt service, laid out two or three Kennedy half-dollars on the table. That courtesy was like throwing gasoline on a fire. The waiters scooped them up, showed them to fellow workers, and all of a sudden, the table was surrounded as if floating in piranha-infested waters.

Wine was ordered, the lunch menu given and questions were answered concerning special dishes listed. As soon as the two upstate New York women took a sip of their wine, one or two waiters came out of nowhere and refilled the glasses. The Kennedy half-dollars continued to be laid out on the table as immediate *pourboires*, and refilled glasses kept pace with the outlay of coins. Four and a half hours later, Mary and her guest, Marilyn, were no longer hungry, and their ability to move about with the same grace they exhibited on entering was gone. It was time to head back for the dinner bus at the hotel. But, there was one more surprise about to take place. A young man wearing a chef's toque came out of the kitchen area and approached the table. He stepped up to the two women and said, "Ladies, my name is Wolfgang Puck. It was a pleasure to serve you today."

The wait staff at the restaurant escorted the women to the door, said their goodbyes and thanked them for the souvenir coins. Once outside the restaurant, there was a problem. Both women had no idea where their hotel was located. A nearby gendarme noticed the dilemma, something to which he had grown accustomed. People going into Maxim's and exiting from Maxim's do undergo a certain transformation. The French policeman walked up to the Americans and said in perfect English, "Ladies, do you need assistance?"

Fortunately, both the "April in Paris" participants wore their wrist bands which spelled out the name of their hotel and its location. The

French officer looked at the information and said, "No problem. I will escort you there." A few minutes later, Mary, Marilyn and *Monsieur le Gendarme*, strode up to the bus, now fully loaded with waiting passengers but minus two stragglers. As the two women boarded the bus, the whole group applauded, and one student in the back of the bus bellowed out, "Did you get lost, Mrs. Sarvey?" Everyone exploded with laughter. Marilyn turned to her husband and said, "What an afternoon! Mary's Kennedy half dollars worked magic among the wait staff. The chef even came out and introduced himself, but I don't remember his name. He must have been German, though. Wolfgang something."

CHAPTER 22

"Non, Je ne regrette rien.": Floyd's Last Hou-Rah!

When Edith Piaf sang this now famous song, she talked about a life well lived, about its heartaches and about its opportunities. She was sorry for nothing, not the good that those had done nor the bad. She was happy with her lot, and looked back at nothing with remorse. So do I. This is how I want my story to end. This is my auto-obituary.

At the time of this writing, it probably would not be stretching the truth to say that blood is still circulating through my body, that my heart is pumping at a regular and healthy rhythm, and that, for the most part, my mental state is at least average. There is nothing abnormal about writing one's own death notice. If the truth be known, obituaries should be written by the one person who knows the most about himself. It makes for a more-interesting reading for the general public, and it is a rare occasion when the deceased gets a chance to read his own summary of life on this Earth.

It is with some pride that my feeling about the status of my country is good. Americans have just elected (two years ago) a new President. There is no shame, no regret that I say, yes, he, Donald J. Trump, is my President. Barak Obama was my President, too. There is no ringing of hands here; I don't have time for such trivia. So, let's begin.

On April 23, 1939, John, my father, and Ruth, my mother, became parents of the only child they were to see live past the age of one month. Survivors of the Great Depression in Curwensville, Pennsylvania, a small town situated along the banks of the Susquehanna River, my mother and father struggled through the war years, too. My father, a tannery worker, and my mother, a clothing mill worker, could never accumulate enough money to own their own home. That, and the stress of other small-town issues drove them apart. It is said that "What does not kill you makes you stronger." Maybe so. But, growing up in a two-room shack, formerly my grandmother's tool shed, with no running water, no central heating and a single electric cord strung from my grandmother's home to the little shack which powered a light in each room, brought no complaints from me. In spite of Pennsylvania's winters, I cannot remember of ever being cold. A coal-fired coal stove in the little kitchen served its purpose. My bed, a discarded WWII army cot, seemed comfortable at the time.

Growing up in a small town in the late 40's and early 50's allowed me to play baseball in the community's first Little League Baseball team. That team, Sanitary Milk, was the first town champion in its first year of play. At the age of twelve, my football career began, and for some reason, most likely because the team did not have a lot of boys on the squad, I played four years of varsity football for my school. In my senior year, my coach awarded me the "Best Blocker Award", helped me gain recognition as first team "All Clearfield County" and honorable mention "All State Pennsylvania".

Three days after high school graduation, I arrived in Parris Island, South Carolina, the Marine Corps Recruit Depot. That experience, thirteen weeks of training to become a combat Marine, was what I still consider my undergraduate education. I served over three years as a United States Marine, and that period of time became my prep school for things to come. Upon graduation from Parris Island, my D.I.'s named me the "Outstanding Man of Platoon 140", promoted me to PFC and sent me to Brooklyn Navy Yard for duty. Three months later, I was transferred to Kaneohe Bay and then to Camp Smith in Hawaii where I served as orderly to the Commander in Chief of the Pacific, Admiral Harry D. Felt. Duty in the admiral's office afforded me the opportunity to meet with and speak to Dwight David Eisenhower, then President of the United States.

In 1959, my high-school sweetheart, Marilyn Baughman, came to Hawaii, and we were married at the First Methodist Church in Honolulu. Honorably discharged from the Marine Corps in 1960, my wife and I found our way to Lock Haven University in Pennsylvania where, in 1964, my undergraduate degree in French was awarded. Turning down an invitation to attend Marine

Corps Officers' Training in Quantico, Virginia, a decision which probably saved my life, I made a decision to become a secondary school teacher of French, and that started what turned out to be a thirty-seven year career in education.

For some reason, the cloud of not feeling worthy floated over my soul and has persisted to the present day. To erase the sense of not being good enough in my chosen profession, I began a quest to continue my study of my target language at Laval University in Quebec, the University of Pittsburgh, McGill University in Montreal, the University of Oregon in France and the University of Grenoble in that same country. Along the way, a full fellowship at Penn State University led to a doctorate in French. That degree finished, I applied for and was accepted as the Head of the Foreign Language Department in the Saratoga Springs City Schools in New York State.

While attending to secondary school duties, officials at Union University in Schenectady, NY offered me a position as graduate-school professor in Foreign Language Methodology. Several of my university students became teachers of target languages later in the Saratoga City Schools.

Largely because my students at the secondary and university level were above average and good learners, the New York State Association of Foreign Language Teachers named me "The Outstanding Secondary Teacher of Foreign Languages in the State of New York in 1984." In an effort to encourage foreign language study and bring that study of such things to life, my school administration allowed me to conduct student tours to Paris, France; Montreal and Quebec in Canada. Over hundreds of students in the Saratoga Springs City Schools were chaperoned and taken to the City of Light, the French Capital. All of my students conducted themselves appropriately as Americans. "Foreign Language Nights" and "French Night", an event of lip-sync singing and dancing on the high school stage, were introduced during my tenure at that school. Some of these activities, at least as of this writing, are still being carried out by my former colleagues.

My wife and I have been blessed with two wonderful children, Brooks and Janine. My favorite son and my favorite daughter brighten our world. In 2015, Janine established the "Dr. Floyd A. Sarvey Excellence in Foreign Language Learning Award", presented to a deserving senior at the end of each school year and honored on stage at the graduation ceremony held at the Saratoga Performing Arts Center. As of this date, four such students have been so honored, and there is room on a plague designed to hold the winners' names for many more.

In retrospect, my thanks go to my God, and my respect to Jesus Christ who, from all that I know about him, was perhaps the most perfect human being. Both contributed to allowing me to achieve to the best of my ability and come to know all the beauties that life on Earth has to offer. Among my blessings is the time spent in a wonderful city, Saratoga Springs. Another is the time allotted me to spend many years with an exceptional woman, my wife, whose life and love enhanced mine in return.

My days on Earth have allowed me to witness nature and realize that God's small creatures want only to live and thrive in their short time on this land, in the water and in the air. These sweet gifts of nature deserve to be protected. I have been blessed to witness the fact that most human beings are good and not hateful, and that they appreciate their own country of birth.

That I am an American makes me proud. This thought has been further reinforced by having the good fortune to have lived in several of the fifty states of our nation. Happy hours, a daily occurrence with my wife (yep, only on days ending in "day") have been a delight. That our way of life, at least at this point in time in the United States, is something which must be preserved is strong. It is up to the American people to protect and defend our Constitution.

When the time comes for my body to take its last breath, my ashes will be laid to rest in the United States Veterans' Cemetery close to the Saratoga Battlefield in Stillwater, NY. On a plaque carrying my name and Marilyn's, an inscription will read, "Hou-Rah!" If my luck continues, hopefully, someone will use a banjo or harmonica and play "The Marine Corps Hymn" from time to time close to where my soul and ashes rest. Semper Fi, and God bless America and the United States Marine Corps.

And, yes, one last thing...Ya should'a been there!

ACKNOWLEDGEMENTS

No book or publishing agents were used in developing this short summary of my professional life. They would have required a more-perfect literary approach. My wife, Marilyn, and my favorite daughter, Janine, were kind enough to listen to most chapters included in this text. This reading of certain passages took place on days ending in "day" and had I known how to use the camera on my cell phone, their pictures, imitating those taken on bus trips in France and brought about by the drone of my voice, would have brought certain chapters in this book to mind and a smile to the reader. And, for the most part, they were there, and that's a good thing. Mack Hawthorne, my grandson, collaborated with me on the design of the book's cover, and for that, I am grateful.

Printed in the United States
By Bookmasters